The Fashion Handbook

The Fashion Handbook

A Guide to Your Visual Image

Second Edition

Sharon Lee Tate

Mona Shafer Edwards

HarperCollinsPublishers

Sponsoring Editor: Anne Smith

Project Coordination and Text Design: R. David Newcomer Associates

Cover Coordination: Mary Archondes

Cover Design: Brand X Studio, Robin Hoffmann

Cover Illustration: Mona Shafer Edwards

Production: Michael Weinstein

Compositor: CFW Graphics

Printer and Binder: Courier Book Companies/Murray

Cover Printer: New England Book Components

The Fashion Handbook: A Guide to Your Visual Image, Second Edition

Library of Congress Cataloging-in-Publication Data

Tate, Sharon Lee.
    The fashion handbook : a guide to your visual image / Sharon Lee
Tate, Mona Shafer Edwards. — 2nd ed.
        p.   cm.
    Rev. ed. of: The fashion coloring book. c1984.
    ISBN 0-06-046622-7
    1. Fashion drawing. 2. Costume design. I. Edwards, Mona Shafer,
1951–   II. Tate, Sharon Lee. Fashion coloring book.
III. Title.
TT509.T38   1991
741.6′72—dc20   90-4547
                                                   CIP

90 91 92 93   9 8 7 6 5 4 3 2 1

Dedicated to our husbands,
Richard Kline and Barry Edwards,
great examples of how men
can look their best at all times.

Contents

Figure Charts

Preface

This book was written for four reasons: (1) to teach you the secrets of professional designers; (2) to help you develop a visual identity appropriate for varied occupations and social occasions; (3) to show you who to save money by preplanning wardrobe purchases and avoiding the expensive "mistakes" that sabotage a master clothing plan; and (4) to demonstrate that the skills and creativity involved in pulling your visual image together can be fun. Fashion should always have an element of excitement and anticipation. It is worth investing time and practice in selecting apparel that makes you look your best, for clothing that maximizes your physical assets helps you succeed both personally and professionally. Remember, you never have a second chance to make a first impression.

There is a special reason you may use this book as a *coloring* book. When you read something, you receive a mental message. Combining this mental process with the physical activity of coloring reinforces the principle being discussed. Use this book when you have a quiet moment, and let your mind imagine various solutions to the clothing problems presented. Think of yourself as the person whose wardrobe you are planning when you color a figure. Trace the figures several times, to try different color schemes. Professional fashion designers create styles by envisioning what an article of clothing will look like, before it is made. They combine art principles with many trial-and-error garments and can envision the potential creation by just looking at and feeling a piece of fabric. With practice, you, too, can develop this imagination and use it to select the most flattering apparel possible.

Begin planning your wardrobe by evaluating your life-style and body image. It is impossible to study your body objectively and to appreciate your good points. Improve aspects of your figure that require improvement. Try to discard prejudices about your body that do not pertain to visible faults. You are a valuable person, and developing an appropriate style of dressing will maximize your assets and allow you to be at your best. Truly chic people can forget what they are wearing, because they have style and their clothing does not compete with their unique personalities.

A unique feature in the second edition of *The Fashion Handbook* is that it discusses many different kinds of occupations and how to dress for each. Most books that cover business wardrobes limit their scope to formal business wear. This is the most difficult attire to understand, because most people are not brought up wearing this kind of clothing. Approximately 4 percent of the working population are employed in occupations requiring formal business wear, yet most books do not consider other types of occupations.

The most expensive clothes you will ever buy are those you seldom wear and those that make you feel uncomfortable. You can dress successfully, and economically, by purchasing garments that are functional, stylish, comfortable, and flattering. Defining your clothing needs by matching them to your life-style and environment will free you to shop with a master plan. You will not be tempted by a persuasive salesperson or lured into purchasing an inappropriate garment just because it is marked down. You will confidently select clothing that fits into your wardrobe plan and is a true fashion investment.

You are not alone in trying to maximize your appearance. Men and women have discovered that looking their best allows them greater freedom to advance into their chosen careers. Seek advice from makeup and hair stylists. Shop in the best stores, even if you are "just looking" and have to purchase more moderately prices items elsewhere. Develop your personal taste, and try creating a new image. Fashion magazines, for both men and women, often do fascinating make-over articles that show a person how to change their image to one that is up to date and professional looking. This could be you. Try it!

Using *The Fashion Handbook*, second edition, should be an experience of self-discovery and creativity. The tricks of the trade discussed in this book will help you make your wardrobe work for you. Remember, fashion is fun. A sense of humor and the self-assurance that comes from knowing your figure and your personal styling formula will free you to look your best and dress appropriately for every situation.

HOW TO USE THIS BOOK

You will need some art supplies to work with this book:

▼ *Medium-wide felt-tip pens.* Select a package with at least 16 colors. The more colors you have, the more variety you can give to your pictures.
▼ *Colored pencils.* Purchase the kind with a soft base, such as Prismacolor.® Buy several flesh tones and 12 to 34 additional colors, as your budget allows. You can color with the pencils and the felt-tip pens, using the pencils for small details and shading.
▼ *Pad of tracing paper, 8 × 12 inches minimum size.* Tracing paper will make it easy to copy illustrations so you can try other color combinations. Vellum or lightweight bond paper will also do the trick.
▼ *Fine-line black marking pen and #2 lead pencil.* These will be used to copy figures from the book for additional style-line or color experiments.

One of the subjects in the book is finding your personal color palette, that is, clothing colors that flatter your complexion. Women also will select makeup colors appropriate for their complexion. Several of the pages have colors suggested; others allow you to experiment with your color palettes. Refer to the color guides on the inside front and back covers for your color type. Remember, some lucky individuals can wear a range of both warm and cool colors. You may wish to experiment with various colors in front of a mirror to confirm those that are the most flattering for you.

FIGURE CHARTS

The figure charts at the back of the book provide solutions to various figure problems at a glance. The first charts summarize the clothing solutions flattering for women with balanced, pear-shaped, and wedge-shaped figures, for several different weights. These guidelines will help people with those body types to emphasize the positive and disguise the negative aspects of their appearance. Next, suggestions for maximizing the figure assets of petite and tall women are given. Finally, apparel ideas for women who want to camouflage specific body characteristics, such as long waists and narrow shoulders, are presented.

Sharon Lee Tate
Mona Shafer Edwards

The Fashion Handbook

Clothing:
The Silent Language

APPEARANCE SAYS a great deal about a person, before a word is spoken. The image you project may be one of competence, confidence, and tranquility, or you may not project a powerful image. Looks reflect your personality, moods, and feelings. Clothing and grooming elicit an instant reaction, and there is no second chance to make a first impression. Does putting this much emphasis on appearance strike you as shallow? How can others judge a person's inner self or worth with a casual glance?

The importance of clothing in social relations has ancient roots. The decorative aspect of apparel was as important in early societies as its functional aspect. Clothes set apart the most prominent people in the tribe. The chief was designated by an elaborate headdress, fine robes, and other rich ornaments. The warrior applied paint to frighten opponents and to declare readiness for battle. The priest's or priestess' vocation and rank were attested to by garments with ritual significance. Through the ages, clothing and ornaments have been used to distinguish one person from another and to declare at a glance the status and often the wealth and occupation of a person.

Appearance reflects who a person is and what he or she wants. Benjamin Franklin once advised, "Eat what you like, but dress for other people." Successful people learn the language of clothing. They learn how to manipulate their appearance to conform to the expectations of their peer group and to generate favorable reactions. They know that first impressions can have a lasting effect. "Look the part" is an expression that focuses on the importance of dressing to your goals and understanding the message your appearance is sending others.

Do not confuse a desirable appearance with physical beauty. A person does not have to be handsome or beautiful to appear confident, powerful, or successful. Appearance is the total impression created by physical characteristics, emotional state, and clothing. Eighty to 90 percent of what you see of a person is his or her clothing, the most important visual element evaluated in a first encounter.

Self-evaluation and an analysis of your life-style and work style are the first steps toward discovering your ideal appearance. Everybody should discover and emphasize the positive aspects of their personal appearance. At the same time, they must confront— and minimize—their physical shortcomings. People who do not understand the nonverbal language of clothing may not realize what their apparel reveals about how they secretly feel about themselves. An unplanned visual presentation often signals failure, unhappiness, or dissatisfaction with self and life. This message is a turn-off to other people.

Consciously dressing to elicit the positive reactions of others is not dishonest. It encourages people to regard you with interest. It invites them to explore the interesting and dynamic person that is inside your well-prepared image.

Learning to Send the Right Message

Appropriate casual dress establishes your visual credibility outside of the office.

YOU ARE INVITED to a dinner party at the home of your boss. It is important to make a good impression, because you hope to be promoted out of a secretarial position. The invitation says "casual," so you select a tailored suit and understated accessories you hope will signal, "I am a serious person: I am efficient and competent." When you arrive at the house, the opening of the door reveals an informally clad hostess in a fashionable pant outfit. Suddenly you feel dowdy and uncomfortable in your serious outfit. As you enter the room, people glance up and determine that you are indeed "serious"—but at the wrong time. This was an opportunity for you to have dressed informally with a flare that would state, "I am your equal. I understand executive life-styles." You have misread the situation and clearly labeled yourself as a person who is unfamiliar with the social environment of the upwardly mobile, a life-style to which you aspire. A person tends to withdraw or overact, to conceal the feeling of being inappropriately dressed for a particular situation. You could have avoided this by researching the event—checking with the hostess about the degree of formality, or asking co-workers what to expect. Business clothing worn in an informal situation diminishes the impact of its authority.

Avoid sending conflicting messages with your appearance. Signaling something that is incompatible with your role in a specific situation will confuse and distract your audience. Clothing is a personal advertisement to the world about your individuality and goals. A successful personal advertising campaign begins with learning what effect your appearance has on others and becoming sensitive to your peers so your appearance is appropriate for specific situations.

People expect the situation and the personality of a person to be consistent with their projected image. Consider the following cases that describe successful and unsuccessful visual statements.

1. A woman wears a tight skirt and a revealing blouse to her secretarial job. She is continually fielding passes from her male co-workers and complains of harassment. No matter how efficient and competent this woman is, others will receive the message "Think of me in *sexual* terms; the work I do is secondary." Her image and her goals are incompatible, and career advancement will not be taken seriously.

2. A bright, young college graduate is stuck in mid-career on the sales staff of a computer firm selling large systems to financial institutions. He favors polyester suits because they are easy to care for. His shirts are usually dark, short-sleeved sports shirts in wash-and-wear fabrications that do not show spots. He won-

ders why male and female contemporaries are promoted over him, even though his sales figures are good. He is not sending a powerful image, and his appearance says, "I am content to remain on the sales staff." His appearance does not distinguish him from the competition as a winner.

    3. An upwardly mobile woman has her eye on a promotion. She carefully analyzes how the people dress in the position to which she aspires, to identify their power symbols. Typically, these include fashionable, well-tailored garments and quality jewelry and leather accessories. She invests in clothing and accessories that give her an executive look. She maintains her good performance and at the same time looks like she is capable of greater responsibility. Her image adds to her self-confidence, and she soon receives a promotion. This woman used her appearance to make a clear statement that she was executive material. Her

image enhanced her feeling of power and competence and improved the reality of her situation.

    People must learn to be aware of the clothing message they are sending, and relate it to their audience and ambitions. The clothing message may evolve as they grow. Differences by region of the country, by urban or suburban setting, and by the formality of a person's profession will combine to influence what is most appropriate to wear. Subtle nuances are especially important in more sophisticated situations. A woman competing in a male-dominated business should evaluate the executives with whom she works and dress compatibly with them. Her position will vary if she works in a female-dominated industry and is evaluated by feminine success standards. Plan you personal advertising campaign by learning to send the right message through your appearance.

Life-style/Work Style

MANY DIFFERENT THINGS influence the clothing that people select for leisure and for work. Geography, climate, affluence, life in an urban versus rural area, and personality are some of the factors that define life-style. Basic body shape often dictates the type of apparel that is most flattering.

Fashion is what is acceptable for a given group to wear at a given time and place. A great variety of clothing can be fashionable during a given period. Traditional and fashion-forward styles define personality; subtle nuances of apparel are recognized by peers, and may seem radical when out of context. For example, a rancher in denim jeans, cowboy shirt, and cowboy hat and boots is perfectly acceptable in rural surroundings, but transplant him to the city and he will immediately be labeled a "cowboy" and probably a Texan. At home, his apparel would be evaluated by its subtleties. For instance, the shape of the hat would immediately be recognized as traditional or high fashion, his boots would be considered "working boots" or special occasion, depending on the kind of leather they were made of. New jeans would be saved for special events, while faded denims would be worn for every day, and a plaid or striped shirt would be considered more casual than a solid-color shirt.

Young people tend to experiment with apparel. They do not have as many restrictions on their clothing and can express their individuality. Often, youthful clothing is evaluated by the society at large exactly the way "cowboy" apparel is: Because it is different, it seems radical.

The single most important factor in determing what to wear is the kind of work a person does. There are four broad apparel occupational categories. Occupations requiring uniforms are excluded, because the question of what to wear on the job has been resolved by the employer or by custom. Formal businesses, informal businesses, service professions, and physical occupations each have a different code of dress. The kind of contact with the public and clients is an important variable in each occupational category. Meeting clients requires a more formal presentation than does working behind the scenes or on the phone. Within each category, a variety of occasions calls for situational dressing, that is, modifications to the basic formula to fit specific business events. Being appropri-

ately dressed for the work situation is more important than being fashionable.

Formal business occupations are those dealing with life and death or with health and finance, the serious and sober professions. This category includes bankers, lawyers (especially when appearing in court), accountants, doctors (when not in uniform), and other occupations that must have visual credibility signaling this person is to be taken seriously. An old banking saying is "Nobody wants to give their money to the Marx brothers." An example of situational dressing in this category is the male lawyer who carefully selects a dark suit, simple tie, and conservative shirt as a courtroom outfit and wears a grey flannel suit to the office. A woman lawyer would appear in court in a tailored

outfit, typically a jacket worn with an appropriate-length skirt, subtle patterns, and accessories.

Informal business occupations include sales, entertainment, retailing, and advertising. Formal business attire is sometimes appropriate in this category, but there is greater latitude to express individuality in dress. Fashion statements are acceptable in these professions and are often valued in creative fields.

Service professions have the greatest latitude in selecting apparel and usually require an evaluation of what is acceptable in the particular work environment to determine how to signal career goals. Examples are education, social work, and public service. An elementary school teacher should dress for the physical demands of the job without losing sight of the fact that he or she is an example to the students.

Physical occupations require clothing that is durable and easy to care for and allows for freedom of movement. Physical occupations often require client contact, and clean, well-coordinated apparel is important. A building contractor is an excellent example of this category.

Formal Business Apparel

ORMAL BUSINESS WEAR for men in the Western world is fairly uniform, and subtleties define the individual's nationality, profession, and location. The most formal businessman's outfit is a dark suit with a white or light blue shirt and conservative tie. Elements of this uniform—the tailored jacket, a woven shirt with long sleeves, the tie—can be combined with more informal clothing to give an outfit more "power."

More women are entering the job market than ever before. Business demands a different attitude and appearance for women who are ambitious and wish to move up the corporate ladder. John Malloy carefully studied the effectiveness of various kinds of apparel for businessmen and -women during the 1960s. In *The Woman's Dress for Success Book,* he advocates a skirted suit in a conservative color, contending that women should not dress like men, but should use the idea of a male business suit to guide them in assembling a work wardrobe. The "uniform" of a skirted suit will give them authority while freeing them from the dictates of fashion and allowing them to focus on an authoritative image conducive to establishing feminine authenticity within the business world.

Twenty-five years have passed since Malloy made his analysis of appropriate formal business apparel, and women have ascended the career ladder and gained new confidence and authority. Conservative apparel is still based on the skirted suit, but fashion variables have been incorporated into the formula to update the executive woman's alternatives.

It is important to analyze the formulas for men's formal business wear to understand the subtle details that define the businessman's suit. There are three main categories of suit cut: (1) the Ivy League suit, or "sack suit," made popular by Brooks Brothers, (2) the updated American cut, and (3) the Continental suit. The Ivy League cut is most appropriate for the fuller figure, while the updated American cut better fits a slender figure. Both are acceptable as formal business wear. The Continental suit is the most fashionable, with exaggerated details. (For example, when the style is close to the body, the Continental suit will be very fitted; when oversized styling is fashionable, the Continental suit will have large shoulders and more exag-

gerated lapel.) The Continental suit is most accepted in the informal business occupations and would make a person in a serious profession look too frivolous.

The formal business shirt has long sleeves and is in either a light color or a pattern. A french cuff is more formal than a plain cuff. A variety of collar styles are acceptable, and the style selected should compliment the size and shape of the face. A necktie is the required accessory, accenting the suit and shirt by adding color (and often pattern) to the outfit.

The combination of colors and patterns influences the formality of the outfit:

Most Formal	Acceptable	Acceptable	Unacceptable
Solid suit	Solid suit	Patterned suit	Patterned suit
Solid shirt	Solid shirt	Solid shirt	Patterned shirt
Solid tie	Patterned tie	Patterned tie	Patterned tie

"Black tie," which designates a tuxedo, is one kind of formal evening wear. A black suit combined with a crisp white shirt and black satin accessories exemplifies three solids worn together as a formal outfit. Translate this formula to day wear for the most formal color combination.

Combining one pattern (in either suit, shirt, or tie) with solids in the other areas is foolproof, especially when using the color of the suit as guide for selecting the tie and shirt color. An example would be a pinstriped navy suit with a solid white or pale blue (a "friendly" color) shirt and a red/gold/navy-striped tie. Combining two patterns gives the traditional formula more fashion elements, and a careful selection of two compatible elements is a must. An example of an attractive two-pattern outfit would be a subtle glen plaid suit with a solid pastel shirt and a small foulard or dot tie that contained one color of the suit. Three patterns worn together compete and are too confusing to create a harmonious outfit.

Ivy League, or Sack

American Cut

High-Fashion/Continental

Most Formal

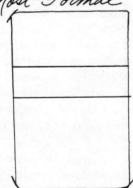

Acceptable

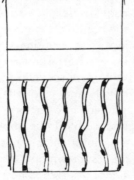

Acceptable

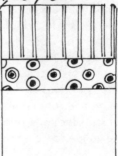

Unacceptable

Informal Business Wear

INFORMAL BUSINESS WEAR is worn most often by people in creative professions, such as advertising, publishing, and entertainment, and fashion-oriented industries, like retailing and manufacturing.

The formal business suit is acceptable for men, but these industries also accept trendy fashion apparel and casual attire that would be inappropriate as conservative business apparel. Continental or European styling tends to incorporate the latest trends in men's fashion. During the 1970s, the European cut featured a fitted jacket appropriate for a slender, athletic figure with a chest circumference 7 or 8 inches larger than the waist measure. Slightly more flamboyant fabric was common. Typical also was a totally coordinated look—from jacket through tie and pocket square and power accessories from custom houses like Dunhill. A banker in high-fashion apparel would look a little too slick to be acceptable to clients and a board of directors, who probably would be more comfortable with predictable, conservative, quality apparel, with no fashion tricks.

A new silhouette was introduced during the mid-1980s, a cut popularized by Giorgio Armani and the Japanese designers. The jacket featured exaggerated shoulder pads and a very slim waist, with a pleated trouser and wider lapels and pant legs. The total look was very similar to the "gangster pin stripe" popular during the 1930s. The subtle influences of this high-fashion look made pleated suit pants more acceptable, and reintroduced more shoulder padding and a looser waistline fit in the more conservative American-cut suit. The exaggerated high-fashion silhouette had a very limited acceptance, but the influence on the market was marked.

The two styles—the fitted Continental look and the exaggerated, oversized fashion silhouette—existed side by side as high-fashion menswear. Fashion tends to evolve in menswear, and change is more subtle and is accepted more slowly than in women's wear.

Informal business wear is often casual. Men can wear winter suits in more informal fabrics like tweeds, the brown family, and slightly bolder fabrications. Summer fabrications can include cotton blends, light-color tweeds, and silk blends. The more casual combination of a dark blazer or sports coat and slacks is ac-ceptable in many situations. A button-down shirt collar is often substituted for more formal collar styles. A darker shirt may be worn by creative types. Loafers and other casual slip-on shoes are appropriate for more informal outfits.

Situational dressing in this category would include the traditional dark suit when a formal business presentation is being made. Informal sports coat and slacks typically would be worn in less urbanized areas, or by professionals who work mostly by phone.

Patterns can be combined with solids by using the same color/pattern formulas as for formal business wear, but several different solid colors are acceptable in one outfit. For example, the navy blazer combined with grey flannel slacks for winter or with tan gabardine for spring plus a pastel shirt and a tie that contains navy is a handsome combination.

Women in the informal business situation may dress in softer styles and fabrics or may wear brighter colors and more fashionable styles, including more fashionable jewelry and accessories. Though the skirted business suit is the most authoritative outfit, informal business attire can include pants, dresses, and sweaters. Situational dressing in an informal business setting is important. For example, a fashion designer might dress in a traditional, dark "power" suit the day she has an appointment with bankers to secure financing for her business. On a day she is meeting with store buyers, she may opt for a high-fashion outfit that features the coming season's most important fashion details and silhouette. When supervising production samples in a factory, she may dress in casual slacks and comfortable shoes.

Informal business situations require analysis of the visual symbols that represent upward mobility. To signal your readiness to ascend the career ladder, consciously separate yourself from the lower-echelon workers. Dress like the people in the job to which you aspire. Your clothing should proclaim that you are self-confident, able, and ambitious, yet a team player within the framework of the established business organization. Emphasize quality clothing that fits and is in optimum repair at all times. Vary your look with accessories that are appropriate and fashionable.

Service Professions

ERVICE PROFESSIONS are based on contact between professional and client in an informal environment. Usually the dress code is implied, not written, and the professional must determine how to dress. Examples of service professions are teaching, consumer sales in nonfashion categories, and public administration. Situational dressing is an important component in this category.

The person in a service profession must present an image of competence that gains the respect of his or her audience. Yet often that person does not have to dress in formal or even informal business wear daily. The formulas for dressing in business categories will hold true for various situations (for example, appearing before a committee, or making a speech, ascending to an administrative position, or attempting to secure a loan from a bank).

To understand how to dress for particular situations necessitates a review of the elements of formal and informal business wear. *Formal business* wear includes:

- ▼ Suits in wool or natural fibers in neutral or dark colors for men, skirted suits or tailored dresses for women. Most "powerful" colors are black, navy, dark brown, and dark grey.
- ▼ Light pastel or geometric-pattern long-sleeve shirts without button-down collars for men, and quality fabrics in well-coordinated, non-revealing blouses for women.
- ▼ Ties in Rep stripes, conservative solid colors, or simple foulards/motifs for men. Women would accent basic garments with appropriate jewelry and scarves and accessories.
- ▼ Conservative accessories (shoes, belts, purses, etc.) in neutral, blended colors to complement the ensemble.
- ▼ Combinations of solids and patterns, with no more than two patterns per outfit.

Informal business wear *adds* the following to formal business wear:

- ▼ Sports jackets with mix-and-match ensembles for both men and women.
- ▼ Softer, nontailored garments for women, more fashionable prints and colors.

- ▼ Less somber colors for both men and women. Women can add brights such as reds or magenta tones and electric blues, purples, and other fashionable colors. Men can add bolder-patterned tweeds and plaids.
- ▼ More fashion influences, bolder jewelry and accessories.

Women in this category can more easily wear tailored slacks. People in *service* industries must evaluate their day-to-day working situation to determine if the following are appropriate:

- ▼ More casual fabrications (but avoid polyester double knits or obviously synthetic fabrications).
- ▼ An unstructured or short-sleeve shirt for men is a very casual business statement. Avoid wearing a tie with a short-sleeve shirt for more formal encounters, even during the summer.
- ▼ Women should avoid sleeveless garments in the workplace, even during the summer.
- ▼ Combine colors and patterns using the formula presented for formal business wear, but you may combine several solids within an outfit.
- ▼ Clean, well-maintained clothing is essential for this category, and dirty or poorly maintained clothing signals lack of respect for the work environment.
- ▼ Appropriate accessories that are clean and well-maintained.

It is wise to keep on hand at work a versatile, dark jacket (and for men, a tie) to pop on over less formal attire when called to a surprise interview or meeting at which you must exhibit authority.

If you are a man in a service industry, avoid shirts and pants in the same color or value, for they might look like a uniform typical of the physical occupations.

A female elementary school teacher might dress in a poplin skirt, bright blouse, and comfortable shoes on a typical day. For parent/teacher night she would select a suit or tailored dress. When accompanying her class on a field trip to the zoo, she would wear slacks, a crew neck sweater over a turtleneck t-shirt in a complementary color, and walking shoes.

The male owner of a small wholesale supply firm would wear casual slacks and a long-sleeve, tailored shirt under a crew neck sweater to work. When selling merchandise to an important client, he would wear a navy blazer, contrasting pants, a striped shirt, and a foulard tie. On the day he picks up supplies, he might opt for denim jeans and a casual plaid shirt.

7

Physical Occupations

THE MAJORITY OF the American population works in physical occupations, yet nothing is written about how to dress for the occupations of that majority. It is assumed that physical appearance does not count in these occupations. Does "dress for success" count for the person engaged in physical labor? Yes! A tremendous number of workers in this category are professionals (for example, working contractors, certain engineers, service supervisors, factory administrators), and many line workers aspire to move up the career ladder as surely as a teller aspires to be a loan officer and then a bank vice president.

So how should a person engaged in physical labor relate to the dress-for-success ethic? First, evaluate the symbols of power and translate them to apparel appropriate for the occupation. A jacket is a symbol of authority, the woven shirt with a structured collar in a pastel color or white signals, "I mean business." A man wearing a tie is more formal than one wearing an open shirt. Add these items to the basic shirt/top and pants when appropriate. Cleanliness and well-maintained accessories (shoes are particularly important in this context) signal competence and authority, for both men and women.

Facial hair on men is questionable, as is long hair. Bearded men who carefully trim and maintain their facial hair will be most accepted. Women wearing excessive makeup and radical or dated hair styles will tend to be regarded as being less competent than their more conservative co-workers. Obvious lack of taste in coordinating casual apparel is immediately noticed and diminishes an individual's credibility.

Situational dressing is crucial for this category. The male building contractor visiting a bank to secure financing for his business would be most credible wearing an informal business suit. But if he showed up on the job in a suit, his client might assume he would not do any of the work personally, and this impression could cause him to lose the contract. The physical professional must determine what image and impression to create for each business situation, and dress accordingly.

A veterinarian is a typical physical professional. A female vet should dress in functional apparel that is easily washed and maintained. She might select washable slacks and a knit top or woven blouse topped with a neat lab coat. Comfortable, sturdy shoes are essential to this profession.

To select compatible apparel, review the criteria for selecting fabrics and patterns in formal business wear. The easiest outfit to coordinate is the one that is solid plus solid. A neutral or dark bottom combined with a lighter, pastel shirt is easiest to coordinate. Selecting the same color top and bottom more closely resembles a uniform, but is often advisable when a person wishes to look taller.

A single pattern combined with solid colors is excellent for building an outfit. When selecting a patterned shirt or top, make sure the color of the bottom is included prominently in the pattern. An example would be a plaid shirt in red, khaki, and forest green, which could be combined most effectively with a khaki bottom and for which a red or forest green sweater would be an appropriate accent piece. Selecting contrasting tops can be trickier, so when in doubt, stick to traditional combinations like red, white, and navy or black, tan, and red.

Avoid more complicated combinations of multiple patterns and solids. When more formality is required, add a tie (in menswear) and structured jacket to a more casual outfit. Maintain your apparel, and report to work with clean, well-pressed clothing, neatly trimmed and styled hair, polished shoes or boots, and coordinated apparel. Make sure you are shaved if a man, and have tastefully applied makeup if a woman. Pride in the service you perform is reflected in your appearance. A rural plumbing contractor billed himself as the "Sultan of Septic Tanks" and arrived to do his job in neat, well-pressed denim jeans, a woven shirt that was immaculately clean, and polished work boots. Needless to say, he was the talk of the community and secured a devoted clientele because his professional appearance assured his customers in advance that his work would be competent and dependable.

As you discover your most flattering colors, build your wardrobe around one color of accessories, to reduce the cost of pulling together an outfit. Alternate footwear, to give one pair of shoes a "rest"—both pair will wear longer when they have a day to dry out completely.

Purchase at least one informal business outfit to have on hand for interviews, and rotate the jacket and slacks or skirt in order to dress up your more casual outfits.

Appropriate dress for
physical occupations.

8

Getting Started:
Organizing Your Clothes Storage

*T*HE OPENING CHAPTERS of this book served to orient you to external factors in society and the work-place that influence how you dress. Now begin to explore the physical and psychological ways to enhance your appearance by analyzing your body size, color, and clothing habits.

A trained psychologist can learn a great deal about a person by looking at his or her closet. Clothing and how it is stored tells about one's habits and tastes, one's priorities and economic status, and one's values and general concepts of sexuality. You can make the same kinds of judgments for yourself. Look through your closet as if it belongs to a stranger, and at the same time define the person based on that wardrobe. Select 10 adjectives that describe the "stranger" you have just met. Compare these with your own goals and life-style. How do the clothes in your closet fit your body and your ambitions?

Think about your goals. What do you want to change about the way you live and the way you look? Gain a sense of yourself and the image you want to project. Set your sights on the next step toward achieving your ideal self-image. A radical change will often make a person feel uncomfortable. Your image should be evolutionary, not revolutionary. Eliza Doolittle's transformation at the hands of Professor Higgins in Shaw's *Pygmalion* made her feel she was a fake at first. The clothing in your closet should be consistent with your personality and physical type, should reflect your present life-style, and should provide you with appropriate garments to wear for occasions you regularly encounter.

Accept your body for what it is today. Many people, especially women, are continually trying to lose the same 10 pounds. The reality is that most women do not have fashion-model figures.* Do not purchase too small a garment in anticipation of losing weight. Tight clothing emphasizes a person's lumps

Newsweek (December 5, 1988) defined the average American woman as 33.3 years old, 5 feet 3 inches tall, 138 pounds, and a size 12.

Before

and bumps, reinforcing the feelings of inadequacy with each glance in a mirror. Look at yourself nude in a full-length mirror and evaluate your pluses and minuses. Work with who you are today. Live in the present, with a realistic sense of yourself. A positive analysis of your figure is essential to applying the rules of design to your specific needs.

Clean out your closet and discard anything that you have not worn during the past year. Donate it to charity for a tax donation, or sell it to a used-clothing store. Old clothes clutter your mind, even if you have room in your closet for them. They may be a sign that you treasure the past more than you value the present. How often have you looked at the jammed rod in your closet and thought, "I have nothing to wear," even though you have spent a lot of money on all those clothes? Write down your goals for next year. Establish the priorities in your life. List the types of occasions you will be involved in.

Consider remodeling your closet, reorganizing the space more efficiently so you have easy visual and physical access to the clothes you own. The single hanging rod is one of the most inefficient uses of space possible. With a measuring tape, determine how many running feet you will need for the following:

tops/shirts   pants

long dresses/garments   jackets

After — Men

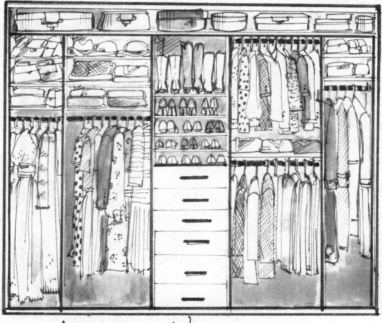

After — Women

Consider the number of garments you have that should be stored folded on shelves. Men usually require more drawers and shelf space because of larger shoes and more items that can be stored folded. Survey your shoes and accessories, and make rough measurements to determine the space you will need to store them. Measure your overall closet area, and experiment with different arrangements of the space you have to work with. Consider purchasing unfinished furniture (shelves, dressers, etc.) to use in the remodel. Doors that open are more versatile than sliding doors, for on their insides you can mount towel racks to hold belts and ties as well as mirrors. You can build your own closet interior inexpensively and easily, or you can contract with a professional closet organizer to design and rebuild the space.

The Bare Essentials: Proportion

T HE MOST BASIC MEASUREMENT of the body, one that does not change unless there is a radical weight change, is the head-to-height proportion. An average figure is between 7 and 7½ head heights tall. Fashion models are selected because they are taller than average, often with a head-to-height ratio of 8 or 8½ head heights. Tall, slender people photograph well because the camera tends to add weight. Asian proportions are often 5 to 5½ head heights. Evaluating your height in proportion to head lengths is an important way to evaluate your proportion whatever your actual height. The sketch below diagrams a 7–head figure.

To find your head-to-height proportion, first measure your head size with an L square. Next draw a vertical line on a full-length mirror with a dark felt pen (easily removed with window cleaner). You will need a partner to help with the next steps. Stand in front of the mirror, with the vertical line centered on your body. Wear a leotard (or underwear) and no shoes. Mark the intersection of the plumb line and your shoulders using the hollow between your collarbones to determine the shoulder line. Square a line for your shoulders equal to one head length. Determine if you have average shoulders by lining up your shoulder silhouette with this line. Wide shoulders will make your

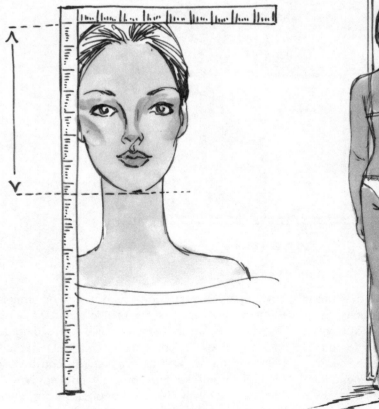

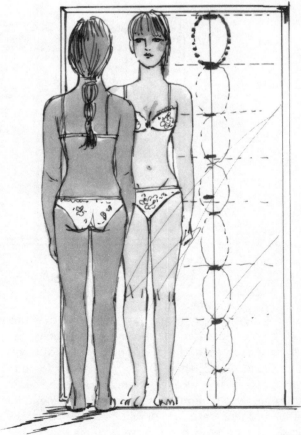

hips seem slimmer. Men with very wide shoulders in comparison to their hip line have wedge (or *mesomorphic*) physiques. Men whose hips/torso are wider than their shoulders have an *endomorphic* body type. This physique tends to have rounded lines. Men whose shoulder width balances the hip, and whose body lines are slender and angular, have *ectomorphic* physiques. Check to see if your shoulders are even. If one shoulder is significantly lower, men may add padding to suits on the low side for balance.

Next mark your waist line and crotch line on the vertical. Mark the top of your head and knees. Measure the space from the top of your head to the crotch. If this length is longer than half your total body mea-

surement, you have a *long* torso. If this distance from your head to crotch equals the distance from your crotch to the floor, your have an *average* torso length. To determine if you have a short or long waist, measure the distance from the top of your head to your waist. An average waist is 3 head lengths from the top mark.

Women should now put on high-heeled shoes (2½ to 3 inches high) and stand next to the plumb line. This will elongate the proportions, so the head–height ratio will be greater.

Fill out the chart as an aid to determining your proportion.

Your Body Type

Total Height (in inches) ☐ ÷ ☐ Head Length   Head/Height Ratio 1: ☐ Proportion
Short = 1:6.8 or less   Average = 1:7   Tall = 1:7.2 or more

Shoulder Width (in inches) ☐ ÷ 2 = ☐ ← compare → ☐ Head Length
Broad = Greater than head length (Wedge)   Broad ☐
Balanced = Equal   Balanced ☐
Narrow = Less than head length (Pear)   Narrow ☐

Waist Length Head Length ☐ × 3 = ☐
← compare →
Less than 3 heads = Short ☐
Equal to 3 heads = Balanced ☐
Greater than 3 heads = Long ☐

Torso/Leg Length Total Height (in inches) ☐ ÷ 2 = ☐ ← compare → ☐ Length of Leg from Crotch (inseam)
Short = Legs shorter than ½ length   Short Leg Ratio ☐
Balanced = Legs equal to ½ length   Balanced Leg Ratio ☐
Long = Legs longer than ½ length   Long Leg Ratio ☐

Waist/Hip Size ☐ ← compare → ☐
Waist Measurement   Hip Measurement
Small = Waist 10+ inches smaller than chest ☐
Average = Waist 9–10 inches smaller than chest ☐
Large = Waist 8 inches or less than chest ☐

Body Shape
Angluar = Long lines to limb and torso ☐
Rounded = Soft body contour ☐
Bulky limbs and torso = Athletic muscles ☐

Posture
Balanced Forward = Head and shoulders forward of hip ☐
Balanced = Well aligned; shoulders align with hip and instep ☐
Balanced Back = Head, shoulders back of hip) ☐

The Balanced Figure

A BALANCED FIGURE has an equal drop (difference) of 10 inches between the bust, waist, and hip measurement. A size 8 would measure (depending on the manufacturer, of course) a 36–inch bust, a 26–inch waist, and 36– to 37–inch hip (measured 7 inches below the waistline). The balanced figure has a well-defined shoulder line. The ideal shoulder width is one head length, measured from the center plumb line. Models usually have wide shoulders to carry clothes and to allow them to drape over a slender body. The balanced figure wears the same size top and bottom. This is the easiest body type to dress.

As a body gains weight, the added weight tends to be distributed in a consistent pattern. The balanced figure would add weight equally at the bust, the waist, and the hips. An extremely heavy balanced figure may add more weight at the waist than at the bust and hips. Large weight gains tend to make a person look shorter, since the size of the body increases in proportion to the size of the head and shoulders.

Have your assistant mark the width of your shoulders on the shoulder line you have drawn across the plumb line. Mark the width of your torso at the bust, the waist, and the hips. Connect the marks to create your "mirror image." Measurements often are misleading, because the flesh is distributed around the body in many ways. One person measuring 36 inches at the bust may have a small back and a full bosom, while another person may have a wide back and a small bosom. Stand back and study your silhouette. Take circumference measurements of your bust, waist, and hips and add them to the chart you started in Chapter 9. Compare these to the silhouette drawn on the mirror. Evaluate your figure shape based on these calculations.

Factors other than measurements and distribution of weight influence the silhouette and appearance of a person. Posture is the most important of these. Helen Armstrong, in *Patternmaking for Fashion Design,** defines posture types: A *perfect* stance vertically aligns

*This is an excellent reference book for the home sewer with a figure problem. It shows how to adjust patterns to accommodate size differences that occur in top-heavy and pear-shaped figures (New York: Harper & Row, 1986).

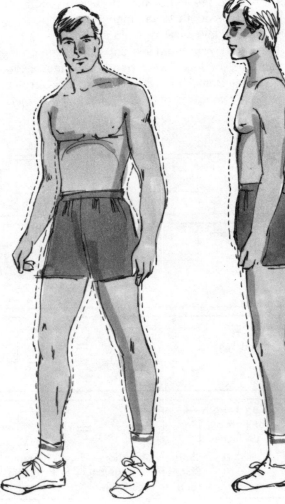

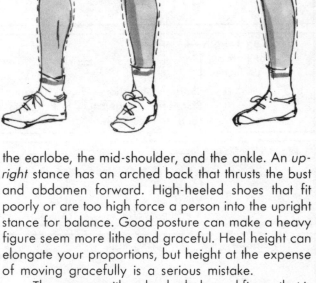

the earlobe, the mid-shoulder, and the ankle. An *upright* stance has an arched back that thrusts the bust and abdomen forward. High-heeled shoes that fit poorly or are too high force a person into the upright stance for balance. Good posture can make a heavy figure seem more lithe and graceful. Heel height can elongate your proportions, but height at the expense of moving gracefully is a serious mistake.

The woman with a slender balanced figure that is proportioned at 7 head heights or more can wear most all kinds of fashions. Even the most extreme style variations will look good on her, and this is the ideal figure for which most high-fashion designers create. As the balanced figure adds weight, clothing should empha-

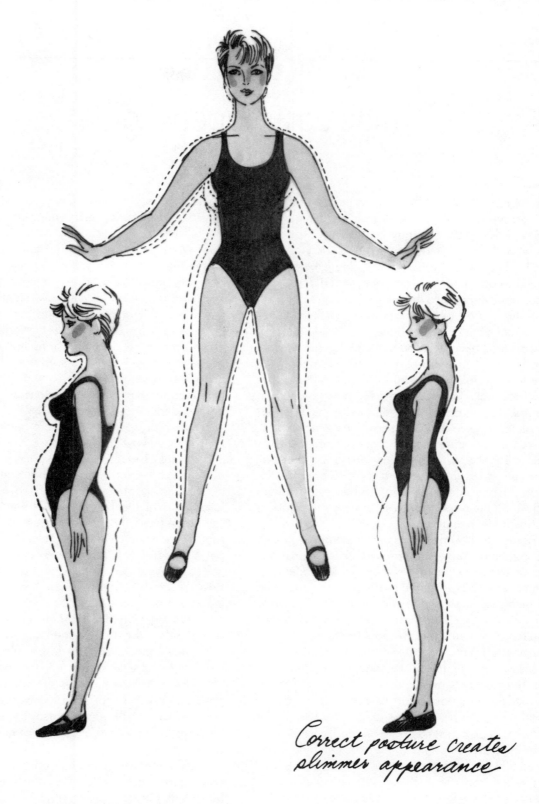

Correct posture creates slimmer appearance

size the vertical, to make it appear taller and slimmer. A very heavy figure will make the head seem too small. A fuller, soft hairstyle helps to balance this silhouette. Hands and feet appear more delicate and are good features to focus on as more weight is added.

If you have a balanced figure, outline the figure above that most closely resembles you. (If yours is not a balanced figure type, go on to the figure types in the next several chapters.) Have an assistant evaluate your posture with high-heeled shoes and then with bare feet. How does your posture affect the total picture? Experiment with several kinds of shoes, to determine the most graceful heel height that still allows you a free and easy stride.

The Pear-shaped Figure

*T*HE PEAR-SHAPED FIGURE has a smaller torso in proportion to the size of the hips and thighs, this figure type is typical of many Americans, especially those whose jobs require little exercise and a great deal of sitting. As a woman of this figure type gains weight, the pear shape is maintained, with a disproportionate increase going to the hips, thighs, and buttocks. Men of this figure type tend to gain weight in the lower body portions but also may develop a large stomach.

Careful dressing can balance this figure and create an illusion of slenderness, because most people focus on the figure from the waist up. Clothes that focus on the face make the most of this figure type. Because the upper torso and waist are usually the slimmest parts of the figure, they too should be emphasized. Bust shape can differ, even though circumference measures equally. Women with a wide back and a small bust should dress in easy-fitting tops, to balance the torso and hips. Many pear-shaped figures have very little flesh on the neck and chest, so a revealing neckline should be avoided.

Focus on the upper torso by wearing light and bright colors, patterns, and horizontal lines. Horizontal stripes can be worn above the waist. Women should define a small waistline with interesting accessories and wide belts. Soft tops, styled with ease, chest pockets, and interesting shoulder details balance the top with the bottom. Women's jewelry should attract the eye to the neck and hands, and therefore may be dramatic.

Visually deemphasize the figure from the waist down. The most flattering bottom for a woman with this kind of figure is a flared skirt or slim-fit pants that fit smoothly over the hips and fall below the knees. This woman's skirt or pants may be patterned in a subdued print or plaid but is best in a neutral or receding color. A flared skirt with enough ease at the waistline to soften the transition from the small waist to the wider hip is a good choice. Hem lengths depend on the shape of the legs: A flattering choice is a hem that falls at the fullest part of the calf so the visible leg is tapered to the ankle.

Pants that fit well can be flattering. A pleated waistline will minimize the curve of the hips if the figure is not too heavy. Pants should be well tailored, with a crisp front crease. Avoid clinging knits, and select woven fabrics. Layering a jacket or vest over pants will minimize the difference between the small torso and the full hips.

Women should select delicate shoes and stockings in the tone of the bottom, to minimize the bulges of heavy calves. Do not wear contrasting shoes or stockings, because that will draw attention downward, automatically leading the eye to compare the size of the hips to the size of the feet. Women should also avoid drop-torso styles and tops that end at the hip line. Wear tops that end above the fullest part of the hip or below the crotch line. Any detail that draws attention to the hips, such as buttons or pockets, should be avoided.

The rear view of the bottom-heavy figure is very important. Always evaluate this figure in a three-way mirror. Make sure that jackets worn over a fitted skirt or pants cover the derriere. Pants should fit without crease lines, bulges, or stress lines. Skirts should flare from the fullest part of the figure without hemline distortion.

Men's suits that fit well will camouflage a narrow shoulder line and a wider hip. Select a slightly larger lapel, a moderately full shoulder pad, and shirts with ample ease. Wear light-colored and patterned shirts with striking, colorful patterned ties. Avoid double vents at the jacket back, for this "pops out" over the derriere and calls attention to it. The heavier pear-shaped man should select the sack-shaped suit jacket.

Men's sportswear should be selected to emphasize horizontal style lines at the chest and shoulder details. Use a strategy similar to the one described a few paragraphs earlier for selecting women's tops focusing attention on the upper torso. Minimize the lower torso by wearing dark, simple styles and neutral shoes and socks.

Examine your silhouette on the mirror image of your figure. If you fit into this figure category, use a red outline to transfer your silhouette to the page.

Additional weight tends to collect
where the body is heaviest.

The Wedge-shaped Figure

A WOMAN WITH A FULL BUST and slender waist and hips has a wedge-shaped figure. This was the fashion ideal of the 1890s, when the Gibson girl, with her full bosom and slender hip line, was the rage. This figure type is still a modern sex symbol, as personified by Marilyn Monroe.

The wedge-shaped figure is ideal for a man, because wide shoulders and a slender hip line is a typical masculine silhouette. Men who lift weights and develop their shoulders and upper torso emphasize their mesomorphic figure type. Men's suits with padding and tailored details such as wedge-shaped lapels exaggerate further a wedge-shaped figure.

Women with this figure type usually like to deemphasize their bust line. They often want to seem taller, because even a woman of average height seems smaller if she has a large bust.

The key to dressing the wedge-shaped woman's figure is to minimize the torso by using receding colors and simple vertical details and to emphasize the hips and legs to balance the larger top. Vertical lines should run not over the bust, but to the side or center front. Avoid decorations at the bust area, such as pockets or buttons. Bright colors and bold prints draw the eye to the area covered, so reserve these for bottoms. Since a full bust makes the torso seem shorter, avoid any design elements, such as strong horizontals and wide belts, that further shorten the visual dimensions of the bodice.

Use all these rules in reverse to select men's sportswear because emphasizing a wedge-shaped torso is an appealing masculine silhouette. A typical knit sports shirt style often has vertical style lines from the chest up, to widen the upper torso.

Women should select foundation garments that control the bust line. Wear a minimizer bra that has been carefully fitted to soften the bust line and contour it naturally. Make sure the straps are the right length, well balanced, and wide enough to avoid shoulder discomfort.

An erect posture is extremely important for this figure type. Unfortunately, many women tend to round their shoulders in an effort to minimize their bust line. Such a slumped posture reflects a negative body im-age and makes wearing clothes effectively impossible. The shoulders cease to function as hangers for the clothes. The visual length of the torso is shortened.

Layering is an effective way to minimize the bust. Full-busted women should avoid tops with a front placket that are meant to be tucked in. Select instead garments that are designed as overblouses and are long enough to create a flattering line. Belt them with a self-colored or narrow belt to lengthen the bodice visually. Vests and jackets that are worn open create a visual path that leads to the face yet minimize the bust area.

The V-shaped neckline is flattering to a full-busted woman, for they direct the eye to her face. High, horizontal necklines are also good, especially when worn with a necklace that falls above the breasts in a V. Avoid wearing jewelry that falls to the fullest part of the bust. In contrast, chokers direct the eye to the face and minimize the bust. Avoid scoop necklines.

Garments that are fitted with darts and many seam lines are difficult to fit correctly, and the dart or seam line leads the eye to the fullest part of the body instead of toward the face.

As this figure type matures, weight tends to collect on the upper torso. Often, the legs are quite slender. Men, as they add weight, may develop a barrel torso, bulky from the shoulders to hip, and their shoulder size will diminish unless they continue to lift weights. Women should select a flattering skirt length to minimize their rather slim legs. Fortunately, men can easily wear long pants to camouflage very slender legs.

Flared and pleated skirts with hip detailing are flattering to this figure type. Slim skirted styles are appropriate, because they give the figure a longer line. Border-print skirts and contrasting shoes draw the eye to the hem and away from the bust line. Softly gathered skirts and pants with fullness at the hip line (soft gathers or stitched-down pleats) balance the full bust.

Block in your silhouette on the mirror image of your figure. If you fit into this figure category, use a red outline to transfer the silhouette shape to the page.

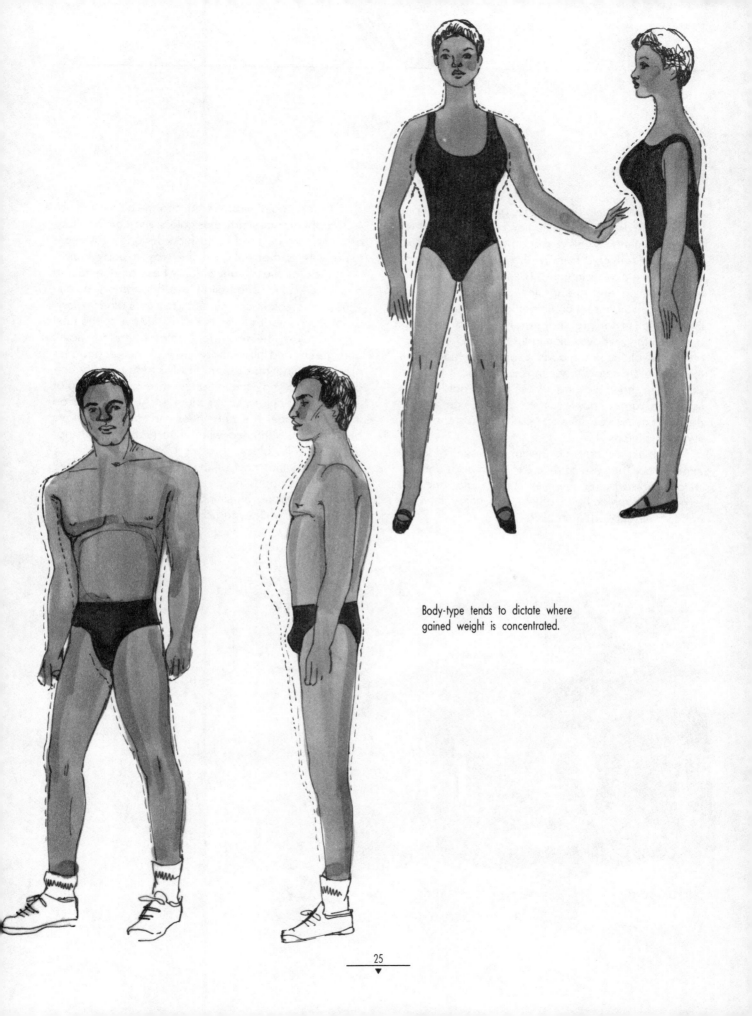

Body-type tends to dictate where gained weight is concentrated.

13

Color

OLOR SURROUNDS and shapes our lives. Color perception depends on a human response to a physical phenomenon. The eye responds to wavelengths of visible light reflected from a surface. Different colors have different wavelengths. The brain interprets the eye's reaction and creates the perception of color.

Color vision is so commonplace for most people that it is taken for granted. Rarely does the average person analyze how color influences life. But colors affect sensations and moods. Experience teaches humans to relate colors to feelings: crisp, sparkling, cold, pure white snow; glowing, warm, yellow-gold candlelight; cool, green, piney forests; dusty, beige, dry, hot deserts. Each color develops both positive and negative associations.

Artists are sensitive to the link between colors and experience. They use color to express moods and sensations. Artists isolate the feeling of a color and reinterpret it graphically so others can enjoy their enhanced perception of reality.

Color creates illusions that change a physical object's appearance. Particular colors and combinations of colors can be used by fashion designers to create visual effects that enhance the way a body looks.

Look at the simple color wheel on the facing page. Red, blue, and yellow are the *primary* colors. These three colors combine to create all other colors. Color the primaries in on the wheel. Move to the next ring of colors, the *secondary* colors—orange, violet, and green, and fill in those circles. The secondaries are a combination of equal parts of the primary colors. The third ring—the *tertiaries*—are combinations of the adjacent colors. Color them in. All the colors on this color wheel are *pure hues,* or colors that have been neither lightened with white (called a *tint*) nor darkened with black.

Notice that part of the color wheel is labeled *cool* and the opposite side is labeled *warm.* Cool colors have a strong blue undertone and suggest calm and serenity, while warm colors have a yellow or red

Black   *Charcoal*   *Medium Grey*   *Light Grey*   *White*

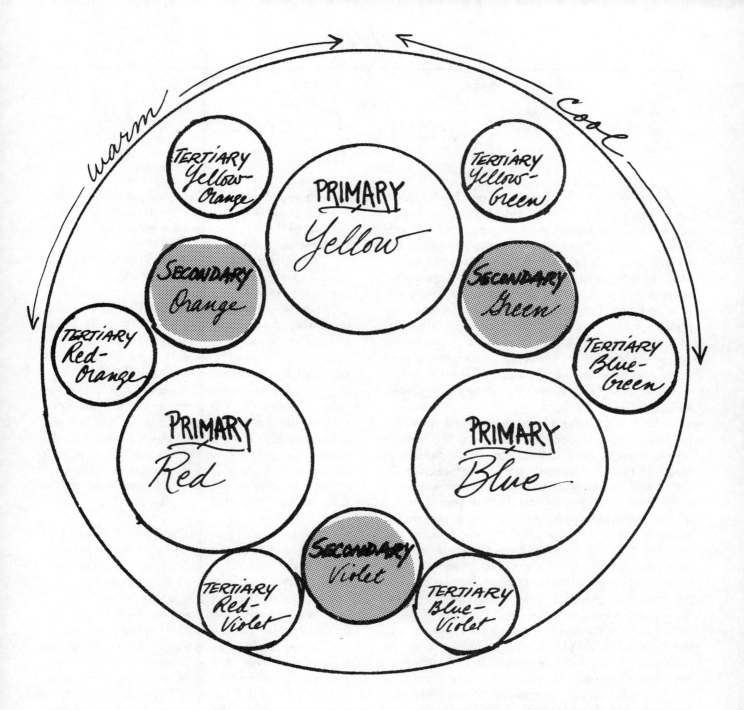

undertone and tend to be energetic and stimulating. Color-related feelings or color personalities have developed through shared, common human interaction with nature and the environment.

Notice also that black, white, and grey are not included in the color wheel. They have no hue, or wavelength, placing them in the visible light spectrum. Yet we can see them. Black, white, and grey (an equal mix of black and white is a true grey) are neutrals. Adding white or black to a pure color lightens it or darkens it—neutralizing the pure hue and the intensity of the wavelength it reflects. Grey may also be made by combining opposite colors on the color wheel in equal amounts to neutralize each individual color's wavelength. Greys made by combining two colors will have warm or cool undertones.

A color can be cool and yet have a warm cast, or warm with a cool cast. An example is red, which can have either a blue-red cast or an orange-red cast. Both of these reds are warm colors, but each has a different undertone that slightly alters it. These colors do not turn grey because the proportion of the opposite color is so small that it affects the stronger hue only slightly without obliterating the primary color's wavelength. This is important to understand when analyzing the colors that are most flattering to your skin tone.

14

Personal Color

SKIN COLOR is basically orange. The pigments are greatly diluted in Caucasian skins to light values, and concentrated in Negroid and Oriental skins to a range of yellow to brown tones. All skin has either a blue or a yellow cast. Skin tones with cool, or blue, undertones include pale pink, cool beige, taupe, olive, and charcoal brown. Cool shades, or colors with blue undertones, are the most flattering for this complexion to wear. Let us call the blue-undertone complexions *moon glow*. Skin tones with a warm, or yellow, undertone, include ivory, golden beige, terra cotta, and warm brown. They are flattered by colors with a warm undertone. We will call the yellow-undertone complexion *sunlight*.

Analyze your skin tone to determine if you are in the sunlight or the moon glow range. Start by sitting in natural daylight, but not direct sunlight. Artificial lights may add a cast to your skin that is not the true color. Do not wear makeup. Wear a pure white garment and a white towel to cover your hair. Look at your face in a mirror. Does your skin have a warm or a cool undertone? To check the color of your body, look at your palms and in an untanned area. Compare this with pure white to determine the true color of your skin. The color chart on the inside front cover contains a simple range of moon glow skin colors. Sunlight skin tones are shown across the top of the inside back cover. Many more tones are possible in each range of complexions, but these will guide you to typing your skin tones. Be careful in judging the olive complexion. It is often sallow, but underneath the yellow overtone lies a blue cast that truly tones the complexion. Warm tones have a peachy or golden tone ranging to a deep brown. Drape a piece of bright orange fabric and a piece of bright magenta (blue-red) fabric around your neck. These colors will react radically with each skin tone. The bright orange will make moon glow complexions look sallow, and the bright magenta will do the same for sunlight complexions.

Now compare your skin color to your eye color and hair color as listed on the facing page as typical combinations for moon glow and sunlight complexions. Notice how hair color compliments skin color to create an appropriate blending. Nature is usually correct in selecting the most pleasing combination of skin, hair color, and eye color in a healthy person. Tampering with nature's selection, especially radically changing hair color without regard to the color and color intensity of the skin, may result in an artificial and unflattering appearance.

A cool skin tone will "fight" hair color that is typical of a warm complexion. Cool skin tones look best combined with ash brown or clear, dark colors. Silver-grey hair with a moon glow complexion is very handsome, and often moon glows grey early in life. Coloring dull or mousey hair to give more contrast and vibrancy is flattering if the cast of the artificial color balances the complexion color.

A high value contrast between skin color and hair color creates a versatile appearance. This lucky person may wear a wide range of colors. Dark hair with light skin or light hair with dark skin is a striking combination. The color of the skin gradually softens as a person ages. Nature corrects the loss of complexion intensity by greying the hair and often softening the color of the eyes, which will stay in the same basic color tone, however.

If you use makeup, once you have analyzed your skin tone you should examine your makeup colors. Makeup can camouflage blemishes, brighten complexions, and give the skin a healthy glow, but it must compliment the natural skin tones.

Skin tone often subtly modifies the color of makeup applied to it. This is most likely to happen, and with unflattering results, if the makeup is the wrong cast for a complexion type. A sunlight complexion wearing a pink lipstick may find the lipstick changing to an unflattering shade of dull maroon. A lipstick color with the proper undertone tends to stay "true" on the wearer's lips. It is a mistake to change lip color to match clothing if you ignore your basic palette, for the effect will not be flattering.

Analyze your own coloring quite carefully, and try to approximate it in the face on the opposite page. (Prisma pencils are excellent for this, because you can lightly color and blend several flesh tones to match your complexion.) Color in your true eye color. Do your eyes change color in different lights or when you wear different colors? Dab bits of your lipstick, blush, and base on your jaw line and double-check the colors to make sure they are the right cast for you.

Moon Glow

SKIN TONES
white to delicate pink
pink-beige
beige - taupe
olive
dark brown, with
olive or blue
undertones
charcoal brown

HAIR COLORS
white
white blonde (platinum)
blue-grey
salt & pepper
medium brown
ash brown
'mousey' brown
'mousey' blonde
medium brown
black, with no
red tones

EYE COLORS
Blue: pale to deep
grey
grey-green to green
hazel & soft brown
deep brown, to
brown black

Sunlight

SKIN TONES
ivory
peach
golden-beige
camel
soft terra cotta
warm brown
golden-brown
dark warm brown

HAIR COLORS
flaxen blonde
yellow, or golden-grey
golden-brown or
blonde
copper-red brown
auburn
red, to strawberry
blonde
red-grey
chestnut brown
deep brown-black

EYE COLORS
Brown — all shades
from golden
to hazel
amber
green
blue with yellow
undertone
blue — aqua

15

Makeup Color

*M*AKEUP, SKILLFULLY APPLIED, will smooth the uneven color of a complexion, accent the natural contours of the face, and highlight the eyes, cheeks, and lips so they radiate a healthy glow. The best advice you can get is from a knowledgeable makeup artist who works with you to achieve a look you are comfortable with and that enhances your appearance.

Three types of color are usually applied: base (foundation) color, contouring colors, and accent colors. The *base* color should blend with your skin type. Foundations are formulated for moon glow and for sunlight complexions. It is essential to start with a foundation that is compatible with your basic skin coloring. Test the color on your jaw line. Cheek color is often too rosy to use as a standard for the foundation you select. Evaluate the foundation color in natural light. The lighting in a store, both incandescent and fluorescent, affects color. Be sure to look at makeup colors in daylight, to avoid distortion and to be able to see the nuances of the color you are selecting. If you tan, the base color you choose may have to be darkened; if you don't tan, it is not changed. Foundation color is never changed to "match" clothing. Sometimes professional photographic models will tint their skin, under the foundation, to appear to have the opposite base skin tone when advertising clothes of a strong color that fights their natural coloring. It is much more appropriate to blend clothing colors with your natural coloring for the most flattering color harmony.

A foundation should even the color of your skin and cover small blemishes. Blend it well into the hairline and under the jawline so you have a natural look. A heavy foundation tends to look artificial in daylight. Base makeup is either water-base or cream-base. A water-base foundation can be thinned and applied with a small natural sponge.

Contouring colors are used below the cheekbones and sometimes on other parts of the face to minimize width or to accentuate bone structure. Contouring colors are made in powdered and in cream forms. They must be blended with the fingers, a brush, or a cotton ball so the color seems to disappear yet leaves the illusion of a shadow on the contours of your face. Blending is essential to achieve a smooth, natural look. Highlight contouring is often used under the eyebrow and at the very top of the cheek. Sometimes, a

heavier foundation or makeup stick will be necessary to mask shadows under the eyes or dark facial blemishes. Applying this under the foundation. Contouring makeup does *not* change color to go with the clothing colors you wear, and it should compliment your basic skin tone.

Accent coloring is the third category of makeup. Accents include eye shadow, blush or rouge, lipstick, and mascara. Accent colors can vary with the colors you wear and are influenced by fashion, but they must be compatible with your color type to be flattering. The secret of accent coloring is to use enough color to create an aura of health that compliments your clothing colors without competing with your nautral shades and looking artificial.

Sunlights should wear accent lipsticks and blush with an orange-apricot base. They can wear eye shadows in subtle brown tones and smokey greys. Subtle green-tone eye shadows are handsome for the hazel- and green-eyed sunlights. Moon glows should stick to the rose-pink family for blushers and lipsticks. Soft grey with a blue cast is a good eye shadow, but too bright a blue is startling. Never wear blue or green eye shadow when appearing on television, for the camera intensifies these colors, creating a very artificial look.

Lipstick shades are most influenced by fashion trends. Very pale lipstick, lighter than your skin tone, creates a peculiar illusion even if it is fashionable. Dark or very bright lipstick can sometimes produce unnatural effects that are harsh and unflattering. Bright or dark lip color works best with a dramatic garment worn by a person with high contrast coloring.

The more makeup contrasts with skin, the more artificial it will look. As the skin ages, makeup colors should be reevaluated to go with the softened complexion and color of the hair.

It is wise to review your goals for wearing makeup. Exaggerated artifice detracts from a person's appearance and is usually inappropriate for daytime. Very natural makeup, on the other hand, can be too light to accent the best elements of your face, especially in the evening. Strive for a happy medium. Patronize a local department store's cosmetic department or visit a beauty salon with a competent makeup artist, and allow these experts to show you how to apply cosmetics to build your skills in enhancing your best assets.

Foundation
• All over face

Toner
• darken cheekbones
• narrow jaw with toner
  if too wide
• highlights under eyebrow
  & top of cheeks

• tone eyelids &
  occipital bone
• blush for cheeks
• mascara
• lipstick

Test your make up colors ~ first at the
side of the face

• Are all colors
  in the same palette?

• Try several different
  shades of lipstick
  to cover your
  entire wardrobe

• Test for compatibility

16

Coloring Your Wardrobe

*P*LAN YOUR WARDROBE like a professional sportswear designer would design a line. Work with colors that are best for your skin color, referring to the colors on the front and back inside covers of this book. Begin by selecting several basic colors for your structured clothes (tailored garments such as suits, jackets, and pants). These colors and garments should form the foundation of your wardrobe, the colors that will combine with many other shades. Notice that sunlight palettes emphasize warm basics like browns, and that the moon glow palettes contain cool neutrals, such as grey and taupe.

Now add fashion colors. Such colors change with the season and with fashion trends, but they are still an excellent choice for the tailored garments in your wardrobe. It is not important to match exactly the colors presented in this book. Rather, use the colors as suggestions to guide you to the palette that will flatter your complexion most. Evaluate fashion colors in a dressing room with natural light. Women who wear makeup should do so when trying on clothes so the colors react to their most natural appearance. Your accent makeup can be changed to go with the newest shades; but, of course, they must remain within your palette. Your shoe colors should compliment your basic colors. A limited number of shoes and handbags in a neutral tone that blends with your basics will pull your whole color story together.

Next consider the neutral colors for tops. Because blouse and shirt colors are worn close to the face, they are usually light colors that lighten and brighten a complexion and link your face to the basic garments and brighter accent accessories. The exact shades of the blouse/shirt colors will be modified by the season. The way the colors are worn will depend on the illusion each person is trying to create to maximize the figure.

Move now to the bright colors for blouses, accessories, and dresses. Such colors can be worn as whole garments, especially in dressy or casual clothes. Bright colors seem more appropriate for soft garments such as sweaters and silky blouses and dresses. The bright palette looks especially handsome in natural fibers such as cotton, silk, and wool and some of the soft synthetics that dye into bright, clear shades. Dress designers often select bright colors for soft clothes because they know these garments do not have to be as versatile as more expensive tailored garments. Dresses are generally worn for a shorter time and do not have to be compatible with a great variety of other clothes.

Play with accent colors. Combine them with basic colors and neutrals. Bright colors add pizazz to the combinations of neutrals and basic colors you have in your wardrobe. Red, with all of its tones, is the most versatile bright accent, because it combines effectively with all the neutrals, black, blue, taupe, brown, and tan. Refer back to Chapter 4, on formal business combinations of patterns and solids, when deciding how to combine several garments into an outfit. Designers often use a blouse or tie printed in several colors to pull together two or more basic colors. This trick is easy to copy, because you can match pants, skirt, and jacket colors to the print to create a coordinated look. Watch fashion magazines and store catalogues for ideas for current fashionable color schemes. They make fashion fun and interesting. You will rarely make a mistake in combining colors if you select all the colors from your color palette.

Understanding your color palette will assist you in selecting the most flattering colors for your complexion. Remember to reevaluate the intensity of the shades you wear as your complexion mellows in middle age. Usually, a lighter, softer shade of the same color will be more appropriate for the softer, mature complexion.

Some colors are not successful commercial colors. They have a limited following because they are thought of as too sophisticated or too ordinary or tend to make many complexions look sallow. Greens, especially the chartreuse family and some of the bright grass greens, are very difficult to wear. Orange has a connotation of cheapness and is rarely used in its pure shade for fashionable clothing. Softer shades of these colors, like peach and olive drab, have more commercial success. Mustard is a difficult color to wear, because it makes many complexions look grey or sallow. Experimentation and awareness of what makes you look best is the essence of successful color selection.

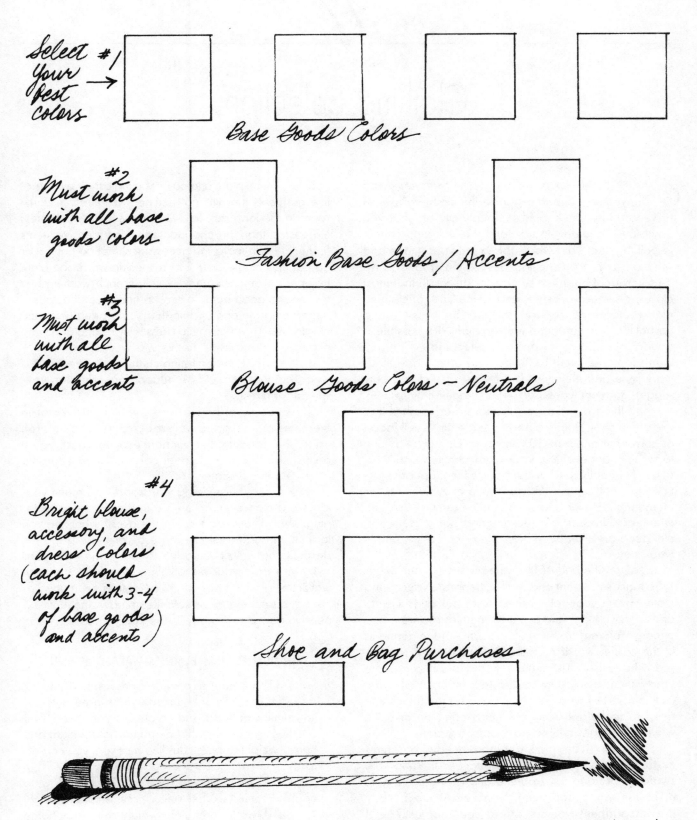

Select #1
your
best
colors →

Base Goods Colors

#2
Must work
with all base
goods colors

Fashion Base Goods / Accents

#3
Must work
with all
base goods
and accents

Blouse Goods Colors — Neutrals

#4
Bright blouse,
accessory, and
dress colors
(each should
work with 3-4
of base goods
and accents)

Shoe and Bag Purchases

On the chart above, color in the basics you have in your wardrobe. Add the colors you want to add— but circle them so you can use this chart to guide your color selection as you color the sketches in subsequent chapters. Use a 5″ x 7″ card to record your best colors in each wardrobe area, as a reference for working on the exercises in the book and to take with you when you go shopping.

17

Clothing Selection

*E*ARLIER IN THE BOOK we suggested that you clean out your closet and organize the clothes you wish to keep. Now you should look critically at what you have saved and develop a plan for clothing purchases to pull together your wardrobe to suit your image and situation. Focus on the job description (formal business, informal business, service, or physical) that most closely fits your work style, and list the kinds of clothing that would be appropriate for your business life and casual life. Remember, many variations are possible in a wardrobe. Each person must select individual garments to compliment his or her figure type as well as work style and life-style. The following sketches only suggest garment types, and will be modified by fashion.

Nothing dates a person more than clothes that are out of style. Subtle differences identify a suit jacket as current or one from 10 years ago. Do not be a slave to fashion, but evaluate your wardrobe seasonally, or at least annually, and discard pieces that are obviously from another era. While you are evaluating, remember that even classic clothes must be replaced eventually. Basic skirts, jackets, and pants are worn, cleaned, and repaired so often that they simply wear out.

Lay on the bed or floor the pieces of your wardrobe that are current and usable. Separate your spring clothes from your fall clothes. Also, put aside casual and dressy clothes and evaluate them as separate categories. You may wish to color in some of the garments in the career wardrobe plans to indicate that you already have them. List any pieces that are missing from your minimum working wardrobe from each job type. Pick the best of what you have, and list the things you need to make the basic garments combine in more ways, as suggested by the wardrobe plans.

Following your plan, purchase needed garments as funds become available. Remember to shop with swatches of your color palette and of the basic garments that you already own. An excellent rule is to buy the best garments you can afford (see Chapters 76–78 for guidelines on how to recognize a well-constructed garment). If you have only a limited amount of money, it is better to buy one good garment than several inferior ones. Also, buy garments you know will complete your wardrobe plan, and do not be led astray by attractive garments that will not extend your existing wardrobe. In the long run, following these rules will be less expensive than purchasing many inexpensive items (complete with matching accessories) that do not last or do not coordinate or fit into a specific wardrobe plan. European women, especially chic French women, buy one or two good outfits a season and several accessories to integrate and update the pieces already in their wardrobes. This is a way to dress well instead of having a bulging closet and "nothing to wear."

We have avoided listing clothes for active sportswear, but these should be added depending on your specific interests.

As you learn how to dress your figure, color in the items on the basic wardrobe chart (Chapter 16), using the formula that enhances your best figure points. Use the 5" x 7" ideal color card you created after reading Chapter 16.

Color in your existing wardrobe, and make your idealized plan even if you are not ready to go shopping. This will eliminate costly mistakes by helping you to think through your purchase *before* you go to the store. Do not let a persuasive salesperson or bargains sway you from your plan. If they do not fit into your wardrobe plan, do not purchase clothes on impulse or just because they are on sale. Remember, the most expensive garment you buy is one that you do not wear.

MINIMUM FORMAL BUSINESS WARDROBE: MEN

▼ **Suits** Three conservative business suits would be a start. If you can only afford two or three suits, select similar patterns and colors. Vary the weights if you live in a climate that demands light-weight and heavy-weight apparel. Buy the best suits you can afford, and sacrifice variety for quality.

Build your suit wardrobe, as finances allow, to approximately six fall suits, three medium-weight suits, and two to three light-weight suits, depending on the climate. For cool climates, add a raincoat with a zip-in lining and a wool topcoat in a color that blends with all your suits (for example, black for moon glows, to compliment charcoal grey and black suits, and camel to blend with sunlight colors of brown, warm grey, and navy).

Suits will last longer if you allow them to "rest" at least one day between wearings. Keep your suits clean, and hang them in an uncrowded closet with adequate air circulation. Make sure to guard against moths and other cloth-eating parasites.

▼ **Shirts**   Select a basic long-sleeve shirt. The number will depend on your budget and how you launder them. You will need at least five if you have them professionally laundered. Select a collar style that is versatile yet flattering to your face shape (see Chapter 43). Add patterned and novelty shirt details (cuffs and collars) when financially able. A wardrobe of 12 shirts in optimum condition will allow for cleaning and repair, as well as a variety of patterns. Discard shirts with worn collars and cuffs. Nothing looks tackier than a formal business suit with a shirt that has worn out.

▼ **Accessories**

Ties   Select at least five in basic colors that compliment your suit and shirt selection. Patterned ties are less likely to show dirt and spots, but examine them after each wearing to determine if they need cleaning. A good basic selection would be two Rep stripes, two foulard or small-dot ties, and one novelty. Build on this basic set as you are financially able, always looking at the tie against your face as well as with the shirt/suit with which it will worn.

Leather accessories   A basic set would include two pair of shoes and two belts. It is vital to purchase at least two pairs of business shoes that will blend with your suit wardrobe. Alternate wearing each pair. This allows the shoe to fully dry out and recover from wearing, which will help it last longer. Maintain shoes carefully, polishing the tops and dressing the edges. A weather coating can be added to leather soles to help preserve them in wet weather. Replace heels and soles when they wear. Well-cared-for uppers will outlast several soles.

▼ **Miscellaneous** (for all menswear categories)   You will need sufficient underwear to have a clean set every day. For colder climates, you also will need undershirts. Make sure to have enough over-the-calf dark socks for a change every day you wear a business suit or slacks. Coordinate them with your shoe color. Select sports socks for more casual slacks and shoes.

3 Suits

5 Shirts

Rain or Overcoat

5-8 Undershirts

Hand-kerchief

6 pair over-calf socks

6 pair sport socks

6-12 shorts

Navy Blazer

2 pairs Casual Slacks

MINIMUM FORMAL BUSINESS WARDROBE: WOMEN

▼ **Suits/Dresses** Coordinate your suit colors so you can build one-color suits (or mismatched suits if they are appropriate for your figure type). Some businesses will not allow pants on the job. Even then, one good basic pair of gabardine or flannel slacks will extend your wardrobe and allow for situational dressing. Select dresses that will give a suit look with an addition of one of your suit jackets.

As finances allow, add medium- and light-weight components to your wardrobe. An excellent plan is to purchase one or two outfits per season that will extend the total wardrobe.

▼ **Tops** You should have five basic blouses to coordinate with suit jackets, in colors compatible with bottoms and jackets. Select one cold-weather coat that has neutral styling and can be worn during the evening as well as the day. Blend the color with other suits and dresses so it is most versatile.

▼ **Accessories** You will need scarves, belts, and ties to contrast and compliment your basic components. Plan these to accent your figure. Purchase at least two basic pumps to compliment your wardrobe. Alternate wearing them, to allow them to breathe, and maintain them (especially the heels) by polishing them and keeping them in repair. For winter weather, add a pair of boots.

▼ **Miscellaneous** (for all women's wear categories) You will need at least two well-fitting bras and seven to ten pairs of panties. If you can only afford the basics, select bras and panties in a tone close to your skin color. Shadow lines will not show as much if your underwear does not contrast with your skin. Many women love to purchase fashion colors to match their clothing when the budget allows. Purchase three to five pairs of panty hose, with at least three in basic skin tones. Add casual socks if you wear sturdy work shoes. Consider wearing support hose if you are on your feet all day. Add a slip and other underwear appropriate to your life-style and wardrobe.

Mix and Match Suits

Five Blouses

Cold-weather coat

Basic Underwear

Versatile shoes and accessories

MINIMUM INFORMAL BUSINESS WARDROBE: MEN

Analyze the work style of the business to determine if casual dress is preferable to fashionable suits. Creative urban professionals can build an informal business wardrobe along the lines of formal business wear, substituting high-fashion suits for the more conservative sack or American-cut suits.

Business style based on casual styling would build on the following basics:

▼ **Jackets/Slacks** Try to have three jackets—one dark, one lighter solid, and a subtle pattern or tweed if appropriate to your figure type. You should have at least one dark suit in your wardrobe.

▼ **Shirts** Select the same basic wardrobe as for formal business attire. Button-down collars are always acceptable in the informal business situation, as are other collar styles. Warm-weather shirt alternatives may include short sleeves.

▼ **Accessories** Select two basic long-sleeve sweaters in accent colors.

▼ **Ties** Same as for formal business wear.

▼ **Shoes** Same as for formal business wear, but emphasize slip-on styles and other less formal shoes.

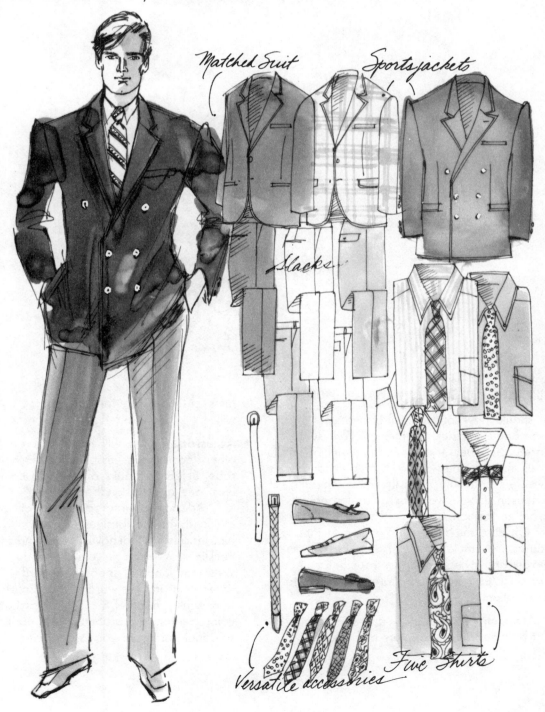

Matched Suit

Sports jackets

Slacks

Versatile accessories

Five Shirts

Matched Suit

Five Blouses

Interchangable skirts and slacks

Versatile accessories

MINIMUM INFORMAL BUSINESS WARDROBE: WOMEN

You should have one formal business suit in a color appropriate to your complexion. Four suits or dresses are basic, select less formal mismatched suits with jackets that may be worn over tailored dresses. Select sweaters and outerwear that are compatible with the season. If you work for a fashion-oriented business, higher-fashion, trendier clothes are often acceptable. Observe the successful women in jobs to which you aspire. Emulate their type of dressing, selecting colors and styles that flatter your figure. Add one or two slack/pant suits if pants are appropriate for your job situation.

▼ **Tops** Have three or four blouses or shirts to compliment bottoms. Select sweaters as blouse substi-

tutes, but make sure they are not too tight, for that will not be considered good business wear.

▼ **Accessories** You will need scarves, belts, and other decorative accessories to stretch your wardrobe. Select two pairs of shoes to compliment at least one quality handbag.

Add to this wardrobe by selecting more formal and informal business dresses and suits, with blouses or shirts that have sleeves and conservative necklines. Women in creative industries should stress fashionable apparel, discarding obviously dated items in their wardrobe and replacing them with quality apparel. Build the wardrobe around color themes, and gradually add outfits to create seasonal variety in your wardrobe.

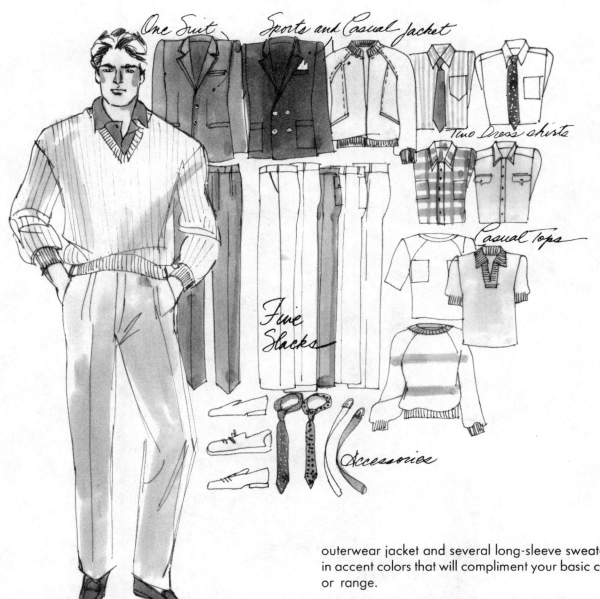

One Suit *Sports and Casual Jacket* *Two Dress shirts* *Casual Tops* *Five Slacks* *Accessories*

MINIMUM SERVICE INDUSTRY WARDROBE: MEN

(Service wardrobes are excellent for college students to use as a guide to apparel selection.) Analyze the successful people in your occupation to whose position you aspire. Emulate their attire, wearing more formal outfits to situations that demand them. Always maintain your clothing, keeping it clean and well repaired. The following wardrobe is most appropriate for the college student.

▼ **Jackets/Slacks** Have one conservative suit and at least one dark sports coat/slacks combination. Select three to five pairs of slacks, preferably easy-care, in a variety of weights and shades. Two wool gabardine slacks and three poplin slacks or khakis would be a versatile wardrobe. Select one casual

outerwear jacket and several long-sleeve sweaters in accent colors that will compliment your basic color range.

▼ **Shirts** Select at least two basic business shirts in appropriate shades to enhance your basic color type. Add three woven shirts with structured shirt collars and several classic polo shirts. Select two long-sleeve sweaters in colors compatible with bottoms and shirts.

▼ **Accessories** Two pair of shoes are essential. One pair should be a more formal slip-on or lace shoe, and the other can be more casual. Both over-the-knee dark socks and more casual sports socks would be appropriate. Several belts would round out the wardrobe. Select at least two conservative ties that match the sports jacket and suit.

Additions would include more variety in shirts and tops, and a second sports coat in a light- or heavy-weight fabric to compliment the original basic. Recycle pants, upgrading worn pairs for those that are newer each season. Select additional casual shirts and sweaters to extend the wardrobe.

One Suit *Casual Jackets* *Soft Tops*

Dress Blouses

One Dressy Dress

Interchangable bottoms

Accessories

MINIMUM SERVICE INDUSTRY WARDROBE: WOMEN

▼ **Skirts/Pants**   Select five bottoms, varying the skirts and pants based on the demands of your work situation. Match one skirt and pants to a jacket for a pantsuit, skirted-suit outfit. This is a minimum wardrobe that should be expanded as budget allows. Select classic garments, with styling that allows you to move easily, and include several pieces that can be washed.

▼ **Jacket/Coats**   Select one jacket that teams with skirt and pants for a suit look. Choose one formal jacket that combines well with your bottoms for a mismatched-suit look and a second, more casual jacket for warmth. Add a sweater in a neutral shade that compliments the basics.

▼ **Tops**   Build a tops wardrobe of at least five shirts/ blouses that work with all your basics. One top should be a dressy shirt (perhaps of silk or a classy synthetic) so you can dress your suit up or down. Add some lightweight knit tops for summer. As your budget allows, build in this area by adding alternative tops in your most versatile colors and some accent colors.

▼ **Accessories**   Purchase a basic, comfortable shoe with a low heel in a neutral shade to compliment your basic palette. Add a simple pump in a plain leather and a medium heel as the first alternative. As your budget grows, add shoes and boots for style, various climates, and style versatility. Select one medium-size handbag made of leather or quality alternatives. Polish it and keep it in good repair until you can afford alternatives. Color key it to your shoes and wardrobe. Add scarves, belts, hair ties, etc. to vary your wardrobe.

Sports jacket   Casual Jacket   Dress Shirts

Casual Tops

Slacks

Accessories

MINIMUM PHYSICAL OCCUPATION WARDROBE: MEN

▼ **Basics** Select five basic pants, in a color theme but with sufficient variety to be worn with a sports jacket when the occasion demands. Add at least five shirts, including at least one long-sleeve shirt with a tailored collar. Add woven shirts, with a variety of sleeve styles to accommodate your activities. You should have at least two solid shirts, since these are more versatile and can be worn most effectively with a jacket. Plaid or patterned woven shirts are classics and can be worn with all bottoms if the colors are coordinated effectively. Remember that pants and shirts in the same color will look like a uniform. Purchase at least one tailored sports coat that can be worn with casual pants (a classic navy blazer is an excellent choice), and team this with

poplin slacks, or a pair of wool gabardine slacks for more formal occasions. In many areas, this outfit will be suitable for all but the most formal situations. For warmth, add a warm sports jacket and several sweaters or sweatshirts. Add outerwear suitable for cold weather as your climate demands.

▼ **Accessories** At least two pair of suitable work shoes or boots, based on the type of work you do, are absolutely essential. Consider safety when selecting the weight of the shoe and the type of sole. A third pair of shoes suitable for wet weather is essential for most outdoor work situations. A casual leather shoe is most appropriate to wear with a jacket/slacks outfit, though dress boots are acceptable in many areas of the country.

Add belts, gloves and undergarments as demanded by the work situation and location. Remember that multiple layers of clothing are very practical. The top layers may be removed as the day warms up, and replaced to stay warm. Several layers are warmer than one heavy jacket, and often are more comfortable. Wear natural fibers next to the skin—they absorb perspiration, tend to irritate the skin less, breathe, and wash easily.

One Suit   *Casual Tops*   *Dress*

Casual & Dressy Tops

Interchangable bottoms

MINIMUM PHYSICAL OCCUPATION WARDROBE: WOMEN

▼ **Basics** Evaluate the demands of your job to determine whether skirts provide sufficient freedom to do the job. If not, opt for pants, building your wardrobe according to the advice for men in service industries. Substitute a tailored dress or skirt suit for the sports coat/slack outfit used for dressier business situations. Women, instead of always opting for the woven shirt, have the additional choice of wearing a greater variety of knit tops that are flexible, comfortable, relatively inexpensive, and fashionable.

▼ **Accessories** Investigate sports bras and underwear, for you may need more support than a normal bra will provide. Comfort is essential, especially in footwear. Do not select shoes unless they provide complete freedom, safety, and support. Select absorbent cotton socks to protect your feet. Avoid wearing neck scarves or jewelry that could become tangled in machinery. To avoid a dangerous accident when working with machinery, always braid long hair or pull it into a ponytail or bun. Consider wearing a smock or other easily cleaned cover-up to save your clothes from dirt and damage. Attention to makeup and grooming will make you look as attractive as women in formal or informal business situations, so do not sacrifice your personal grooming standards because you work in a physical industry. Select a sturdy, roomy handbag. To hold money, lipstick, and credit cards, you might slip into the handbag a small shoulder bag that can be pulled out to wear when you need mobility.

18

Fashion Colors

*J*UST AS A DESIGNER beginning a line must consider many factors before final color selection is made, so are there many things you must consider in choosing colors for your personal wardrobe.

1. *Season.* Certain colors are generally considered appropriate for different times of the year and different climates. Summer and spring colors tend to be lighter and brighter than the dark, rich fall and winter colors, but darks and lights are found in each season's palettes. Imagine walking down a city street in the middle of a winter day dressed in a white outfit. You would look quite conspicuous, because white is not a seasonal color for winter street wear. White in the winter evening would be more acceptable, especially for a formal evening or at home.

2. *Category of merchandise.* Classic, tailored clothing usually comes in basic colors that will endure for several seasons. Brighter novelty colors are chosen for casual clothing and evening wear. Designers tend to use experimental colors and prints more in dresses than in tailored jackets and shirts, because dresses are not expected to last as long and do not have to coordinate with other pieces. Men's sportswear can be very colorful, but use of vibrant colors for business suits would be inappropriate.

3. *Area of the country.* City clothing tends to be more sophisticated in coloring, favoring darker colors and neutrals. Clothing worn in sun-belt climates tends to be brighter and lighter in color, because of the predominance of casual, warm-weather clothing. Traditional casual clothing, popular in the south and east, for spring typically has a bright palette of hot pink, grass green, navy, and yellow.

4. *Life-style.* Merchandise designed for formal and informal business wear is more conservative in style and color than casual sportswear that can be worn for leisure or more informal work situations. Business attire is more neutral in color so it does not detract from the personality and role of the worker. Savvy business people can use color to emphasize their image. For example, a businesswoman giving a speech in a red blazer will hold the attention of the audience, and a man in a dark navy or black suit will have a more powerful image than one in a light grey suit.

5. *Price.* More expensive garments tend to come in more sophisticated colors. This does not mean they are darker or lighter than moderately priced apparel, only that they have more unusual and innovative color combinations. Expensive, high-fashion apparel reflects European trends more quickly than moderately priced clothing. Colors for less expensive clothes tend to be more conservative and repeat the colors that sold best in expensive garments after they have become more familiar to the general public.

6. *Wearability.* A successful color must flatter a person. Designers often include both blue-based and warm-based colors so that each palette will have a choice of flattering colors. Young people tend to be

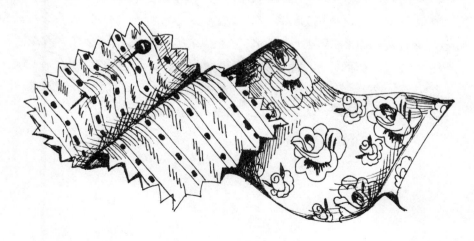

more experimental, wearing trendy colors with less concern as to how flattering they are, because they do not have to conform to the dress codes implied in most business or social situations.

7. *Variety.* Designers constantly change the colors in their lines, because color is a powerful motivator that encourages people to purchase new clothing. A customer will not purchase five pairs of navy pants each season. Color variety encourages additional sales by giving the customer a greater array of merchandise from which to choose.

8. *Fabric.* Color reacts differently on different fabrics. Colors that are deep and rich on a fabric with a shiny surface can be quite dull and uninteresting on a matte-finish fabric. Always evaluate a garment from two perspectives: close up, to see how it effects your complexion; and from a distance, to determine the total effect. Shiny surfaces can make a body seemer larger. Tweeds often have a different cast from a distance. These examples demonstrate how important it is to look at the whole picture when purchasing a garment.

9. *Color predictions.* The earliest color predictions for the designer and retailer come from a consortium of people involved in fashion, home furnishings, color psychology, and trend reporting. The "color think-tank" evaluates world trends and distills them into commercial color lines for all product manufacturers that subscribe to their color report. Colors are popular in predictable cycles, and this gradual evolution of popular colors greatly influences the use of color in manufactured products.

When you pick colors for your personal wardrobe, many of these factors will influence you. Is the color appropriate for when and where you will be wearing the garment? Does it reflect quality and fashion? Whatever else you consider, remember that your highest priority should be to choose colors that flatter you and are compatible with your image and situation.

Use 3x5" file cards—cut tiny swatches out of the seams of your existing wardrobe, and tape, pin, or staple to card. Use card to select prints and additional pieces for your wardrobe. Make another card with swatches of your most flattering colors. Do not look for exact matches. Use card to select the color range best suited for you.

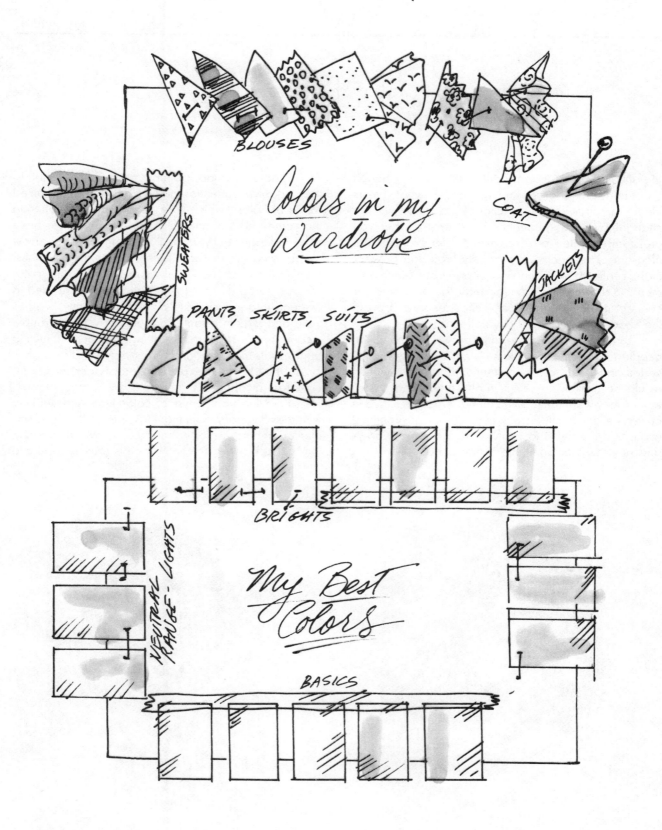

BLOUSES

Colors in my Wardrobe

COAT

JACKETS

SWEATERS

PANTS, SKIRTS, SUITS

BRIGHTS

My Best Colors

NEUTRAL RANGE - LIGHTS

BASICS

19

Color Profiles

COLORS AFFECT PEOPLE differently. Even though there are shared feelings about what colors mean, an individual's reaction to a color will be changed by past experiences. For example, when you are complimented on a particular red sweater, this pleasant experience will probably lead you to wear that sweater more often and to purchase other garments in that color. A person may tire of a color or connect it with an unpleasant experience and avoid the shade even though it is flattering.

Environment, life-style, and personality condition people to like specific colors. A person who is introverted and wants to avoid attention and confrontation would be unlikely to select bright, advancing colors, even if they were the most flattering. A person raised in an exuberant family in a warm, casual environment might find it difficult to conform to the somber greys and neutrals that dominate business apparel.

People develop clothing personalities; that is, they adopt a particular kind of apparel or a limited range of colors, which may, in fact, be less flattering than others. The traditionalist, for example, may have a limited palette for casual clothing and a narrow range of navy, grey, and taupe for "serious" clothes. Breaking out of the usual clothing type and color range may be difficult for this person. People used to wearing informal sportswear that fits loosely, washes well, and is comfortable to wear may have trouble wearing more structured clothing. For them, selecting appropriate colors and patterns may be difficult because they lack the experience necessary to coordinate formal apparel.

Knowing your physical color type and working with the range of colors that looks best with your complexion and hair color is the first step toward selecting the best color environment, for both your apparel and

Warm/sunlight skin tone.

Cool/moon glow skin tone.

Warm/sunlight skin tone.

Cool/moon glow skin tone.

living space. Understanding your color personality and why you prefer certain colors is the second step. To know yourself is often difficult. But it is important to define your personality type and to recognize whether you desire to blend in with the crowd or to stand out. Remember that the sunlight and moon glow shades are a *suggested* range of colors that will flatter your complexion, but they are not the only colors that are flattering. Experiment to find your own unique blend of colors, personality, and style.

A third step toward finding a suitable color environment is understanding the characteristics that colors have quite apart from how they affect you. Colors have unique personalities, with positive and negative sides. Many colors have a different impact when worn by women than by men. Such considerations will also influence when a particular color is selected and who selects it. The following 11 chapters profile individual colors.

20

Red

RED IS THE FIRST COLOR to which a baby responds. It is warm, romantic, sensual, and aggressive. Red rooms make food look appealing and encourage eating. Red increases a person's pulse and awareness of surroundings. The positive associations of red include Christmas and Valentine's Day. Red is the color of the traditional bridal sari in India. The negative aspects of red center on its association with heat and with the devil.

Red is an advancing color, a color to be noticed. It is often worn by positive, extroverted personalities. Red focuses attention on the part of the body it covers. In its large range of shades and tones, red blends with many colors and acts as a bright neutral. It is the most versatile accent color and is a component of many traditional color combinations, such as nautical navy, red, and white, a favorite spring color story. Red and brown is a high-fashion combination, while red combined with black, grey, khaki, taupe, or white makes classic color combinations.

Red is a power color when worn in small doses with neutral and dark suits for men and women's formal business wear. The red tie, or red combined with other colors, is a classic because it focuses attention on the wearer's face and enhances a natural, healthy complexion. Red combines well with all the traditional formal suit colors (navy, black, grey, khaki, and tan).

Red is versatile, and handsome shades of blued-red and warm, orange-cast red can be worn effectively by both moon glow and sunlight complexions. Red in apparel or in a room reflects a person's complexion. Because rosy cheeks are associated with health, the red reflections make a person with a high-contrast complexion seem healthy. Bright red close to the face of a person with a sallow or florid complexion may overwhelm that person's look or make them seem flushed.

Men wear red effectively as an accent color. Ties and pocket squares in bright or subtle tones of red are handsome accessories. Red in casual wear brightens neutrals or darks well. Men should avoid wearing too much red in one outfit. It should be saved for accents, like the bright element in a plaid, a print, or a sweater, or as a surprise accent in a sock or argyle pattern.

Women can use red as either an accent color or a fashion statement. A red dress stands out in a crowd but may seem frivolous at a formal business event. A red tailored blazer focuses attention on the wearer, and has a more formal look when worn with a tailored dark skirt. Red shoes and handbags call attention to the wearer's feet (and hips if it's a shoulder bag hanging at the hip).

Red is a versatile, power color that may be worn effectively by men and women of all ages.

21

Pink

*P*INK IS A UNIQUE COLOR, not just a softer version of red. Pink is a feminine color, though it is also a fashion color for men. Pink is associated with a delicate, nonaggressive, yet pleasing personality. When pink is used to package food or beauty products, people perceive the product as tasty or effective. Bakery boxes colored in soft pink make us anticipate the delicious cake we know is inside.

A mid-tone pink called *Baker-Miller pink* (the color of Pepto-Bismol), named after the doctors who discovered its calming attributes, actually subdues a person's actions for a limited time. This color physically inhibits the secretion of adrenalin. Being placed in a Baker-Miller pink room seems to calm people suffering from anxiety or hyperactivity, as if they were chemically sedated. Pink has been the traditional nursery color for girls—perhaps bringing out a more passive personality.

Fashion forward men wear pink oxford shirts with navy, black, or dark grey suits for informal business wear. Pink sweaters and accent accessories are a handsome contrast to dark skin tones. Madras plaids are popular men's shirtings and often have pink blocks.

Wearing pink close to the face gives the skin a rosy, healthy glow. Blue-based pinks are flattering to moon glow skins. Worn with somber greys and authoritative navy, pink flatters the complexion and softens tailored business clothing. Sunlight complexions should wear pink with a yellow cast, such as watermelon shades with their warm undertones.

22

Orange

ORANGE APPEALS TO MANY PEOPLE. Orange inspires activity. These two traits make orange a favorite color for uniforms and for the interiors of fast-food restaurants that want to attract everyone yet serve them rapidly.

Ironically, orange is sometimes used in casual clothing, though it is not a very popular seller. Perhaps full-strength orange "fights" the diluted orange of Caucasian skin. Positive associations with warmth and sunsets have not enhanced orange's overall popularity for apparel. Red-orange is handsome on tanned sunlight complexions and dark brown skins.

When softened, orange turns into peach, apricot, and coral. Men like to see these colors on women, for they have an elegant feeling that is light and feminine but are somehow not as frivolous as pink. The soft corals and peaches are effective, sophisticated, yet flattering backgrounds for intimate rooms like bedrooms and bathrooms. They are popular colors for intimate apparel and at-home clothing. These colors softly enhance the natural warmth of sunlight complexions and substitute for the pink shades that are more effective on moon glow skin. These shades are the typical highlighters used for sunlight accent makeup.

Deepened and toned down with brown into rust and terra cotta, the orange color family has a traditional place in the fall palette. Rust is particularly appropriate for sunlight complexions. (The alternative for moon glows would be the burgundy-grape family, equally popular as a fall color.)

Menswear uses orange as an accent color and a foil to brown formal wear. Tie patterns often will incorporate orange to give "punch" to a somber brown pattern. Pale orange shirts are a fashion novelty, and may be worn for summer sportswear. Rust is an accent popular in informal fall menswear for sweaters and accent accessories.

23

Brown

ROWN IS A NO-NONSENSE COLOR, the perfect foil for sturdy country clothes in the many shades of camel through chocolate. Brown is a sincere and popular color for men, though it tends to be more casual than grey, navy, and black, and is therefore worn less for serious business apparel. Former President Ronald Reagan wore brown business suits and legitimized them for more formal business occasions. Browns in tweeds and textured suiting borrowed from menswear are quite appropriate for tailored women's city garments and business wardrobes.

The brown family, ranging from pale tans to deep, dark chocolate browns, is a staple in men's casual wear. Brown accessories are acceptably worn with brown and navy casual and formal outfits. Chocolate brown combined with white has a crisp, warm-weather look. Tan, khaki, and beige also are appropriate spring colors, especially when teamed with pastels and white.

The other side of the brown personality is that it can appear dirty and dull. Eastern Europeans still connect brown with the oppressive uniforms of the Nazis. This negative association has been passed down to generations who never experienced Nazi oppression.

Brown when softened develops into two tones—taupe (a cool beige) and camel (a warm beige)—that make it appropriate for both moon glow and sunlight complexions. Taupes, or greyed browns, flatter the moon glow complexion. Taupes are neutrals that combine with many brilliant colors and black and white, combinations that make taupe a year-round color. Camel flatters sunlight complexions. It combines with red, cream, black, and deep brown to create rich, easy-to-live-with outfits that have a casual feeling. Combined with grey, taupes and camels are an elegant business color package for working women.

24

Green

GREEN IS A COLOR that surrounds us in nature and has a cool, comfortable appeal. It is a calm, neutral color when lightened and dulled. Pale green is often used as a background for hospital rooms.

Bright grass green, chartreuse, and many of the olive hues do not sell well in apparel. They seem to bring out sallow tones in many sunlight complexions and clash with the blue undertones of moon glows.

Tones of green that retail well for apparel are the blue-greens, such as teal, aqua, and turquiose, colors that are more flattering to most complexions. Turquoise is an advancing shade that accents many neutrals effectively. Dresses, tops, and sweaters often are styled in these upbeat colors.

Hunter or forest green appeals to less than 3 percent of the population, yet it has the reputation of being a classy color. In combination with white, hunter green is often used in interiors for a clean, well-bred elegance, and it has the same feel in apparel. It is found in many tartan shades and has appeal for people of English-Scottish ancestry. Hunter green is a masculine shade, and green as an accent color is appropriately worn with shades of navy, black, and the taupe and tan families in menswear. Green is also a traditional color for men's casual golf clothes. Bright green and the range of aquas and teals are popular casual knit shirt colors.

Green neutralized and softened to olive drab, commonly called "OD" in the fashion industry, is a neutral that rivals camel and beige. The ease with which it combines with brights makes it more versatile than other shades of green. Although widely used, it is really most flattering on a vibrant, high-contrast sunlight complexion, especially a person with green or hazel eyes. OD can bring out the sallow undertones of many complexions.

Olive green is a reminder of war and is often adopted by the very young as they fantasize about warfare. Camouflage patterns are often in fashion for teenage boys.

25

Blue

*B*LUE IS THE FAVORITE COLOR of the majority of adults. Navy blue has power, authority, and dignity because of its long association with police and military dress uniforms. Navy and white are crisp nautical colors.

"Cardiac blue," a soft, pale blue, is used in hospital intensive care rooms because of its calming effect. It is a natural tranquilizer, but it is not the physical depressant that Baker-Miller pink is.

Blue is usually not associated with eating, because it is not a natural food color and does not enhance the color of red meats and foods. The most positive food association is with the crisp cleanliness of a traditional blue and white Scandinavian kitchen. Few successful restaurants are in blue.

This cool, versatile color is the predominant shade of society's apparel. This is especially true of the blue "Mao suit" in mainland China, but a look over a crowd of Westerners will prove that blue dominates their color palette also.

Navy is one of the most versatile neutral-darks. It is a power color for both men and women and is appropriate for formal business wear as well as for all categories of casual apparel. The moon glow complexion can wear inky, dark navy. Sunlights should select a clear, bright navy to wear close to the face. Navy is a versatile neutral and combines with many brights, neutrals, and pastels. It is the typical spring dark color, and looks good with both white and off white. Women wearing navy should stick to navy accessories, or accent an outfit with a neutral or bright, such as white or red. Avoid wearing black accessories with navy. Men may combine black or brown accessories with navy suits, with black being the more formal choice.

The navy blazer is a classic component of a man's wardrobe. It is versatile and accepted in many business and social situations. Teamed with grey flannel or taupe, tan, or camel gabardine slacks, it makes a perfect winter outfit. The navy blazer is equally acceptable as a warm-weather outfit when worn with white or tan cotton twill pants. Women can duplicate this look, wearing the navy blazer over pants or a skirt for a versatile business suit.

The blue chambray shirt is another classic component of a man's wardrobe. This shirt is slightly more casual than a white or off-white shirt, and has a "friendly" look. It is appropriate for the most formal business situations. It combines well with navy, black, and dark grey business suits. Newscasters and television personalities often wear a blue shirt, because it is more flattering on film and on videotape; this has made it even more popular.

Denim blue, in all its variations, has done a great deal to change Western society into a blue-based apparel society. Blues in many shades, from the warm cobalts and turquoises that flatter sunlight complexions to the greyed blues and soft periwinkles that are so appropriate for moon glow complexions, appear repeatedly in fashion apparel and interiors.

Purple

HISTORICALLY, PURPLE symbolized wealth and royalty, because it was very expensive to produce from natural dyes.

Purple is difficult to combine with other colors. It is more popular with women than with men. It remans an exotic color that is used sparingly in fashion, although it does have specific fashion cycles and is sometimes very popular. Purple is a handsome color for people with deep brown skins. A warm red-violet compliments a sunlight tanned complexion. Blue-purple is effective on moon glow skins.

Purple is an accent color in menswear and occasionally is a fashion color in sports tops, casual summer shirts, and sweaters. It is a good accent color in tie prints, because it is a nice contrast to brown, tan, black, grey, and navy. Purple sometimes is used as an accent color in sweaters and argyle knit patterns.

Lavender—purple lightened with white—has the connotation of delicate old age. Occasionally, lavendar surfaces as a chambray shirt color for fashionable menswear.

Orchid is a red-based, light purple that is rejected by many people because it does not combine well with most skin tones. Orchid in large doses can increase feelings of illness and nausea.

27

Yellow

YELLOW, BECAUSE OF THE LENGTH and intensity of its color waves, is the first color to be processed by the eye, and so it is a highly visible color. When used in small amounts in dark prints, it makes them "pop," or seem more lively. Yellow is a frequent accent color for men's tie prints. Bright yellow is often found in high-visibility clothing, such as sailing wear (so someone washed overboard can be easily spotted) and uniforms for highway workers.

Yellow is the most schizophrenic color in the palette. On the positive side, it seems sunny, clean, and fresh. As the dominant color in an outfit or environment, it has a negative effect on people's emotions. Yellow tends to create anxiety and encourage negative responses. It inhibits minor muscle movement, and persons tend to lose control of their temper more readily in yellow surroundings. The teachers and parents in a local nursery school were very proud of the sunny yellow paint job they gave the classrooms, until the children moved in. The children quarreled more and often burst into tears. When the rooms were repainted a soft blue, the anxiety level of the youngsters was greatly reduced and harmony was restored.

Time tends to pass more slowly in a yellow room. Imagine looking over the hood of a yellow car while you are stuck in traffic. It could be a traumatic experience, especially if you then return home to a yellow kitchen.

Yellow and black is a warning-color combination. Because of yellow's high visiblity, signs warning of detours or road work are yellow and black. This combination also occurs in nature as a warning. It declares the stinging potential of bees, wasps, and yellow jackets.

Pale yellow chambray shirts are very popular for menswear. They blend well with all the dark colors traditionally found in tailored suits. Ties with yellow grounds are a fashion item, but have a similar effect as red grounds, because they focus attention on the face due to the intensity of yellow's color rays. Gold is an alternative to red in nautical navy and white color schemes and is a classic with black and white. The yellow range is popular for men's knit sport shirts.

Yellows are more flattering to sunlight complexions than to moon glow tones, but they should always be carefully evaluated before being worn next to the face. Yellow accents are effective, but the color is overwhelming as a total outfit. Yellow is a popular bathing suit color. The bright range contrasts nicely with brown skin tones and enhances a tan.

Yellow retains its physical impact even when diluted with black or white. Mustard tends to make complexions look rather sallow and is generally unflattering to both sunlight and moon glow color types.

Pale Yellow

Gold

28

Black

*I*N SCIENTIFIC TERMS, black is not a color at all. It is the absence of any colored light reflecting from a surface. But in the vernacular we call it a color. Black is associated with somber events and death—it is the color of mourning. Because black absorbs heat, it may have negative associations in a warm climate.

Despite its negative aspects, black is a versatile clothing color. Black apparel may be sophisticated, powerful, and sexy. Black neutralizes shape and makes a person seem slimmer. When confined to the lower part of the body, black can be worn by every complexion tone. Black combines so well with lights and brights that excluding it from your wardrobe would eliminate the most versatile neutral. It is an effective bathing suit color because it provides contrast to a tan skin.

Black is a classic formal color for men's tuxedos. Many experts feel a man is never more handsome than in a black tuxedo and white shirt. Because of this long tradition, black and white is a formal color combination. A black suit with a white tie is a more powerful combination than a grey pinstripe and blue chambray suit, though this combination is also more foreboding and less "friendly." Black accents grey and brown effectively, and is a basic accessory color for menswear. Black mixed with tan or beige is more informal, because some of its impact has been diluted.

More thought must be given to wearing black next to the face than other colors. Black is most attractive to moon glows and sunlights that have a high-contrast complexion. High contrast means hair that is significantly lighter or darker than the skin. When black is worn close to the face, use bolder accent makeup. Black is unattractive on a dark brown or sallow skin. Black, dark brown, and dark navy do not provide enough contrast to flatter these complexions. Black enhances the pallor of a sallow or pale complexion. Wearing a black jacket with a contrasting shirt or top is an effective way to soften the effect, because the light color will reflect in the face and highlight the complexion. Even people with high color should avoid wearing black when they are tired and drawn.

29

Grey

GREY IS A SOPHISTICATED neutral that has authority and a businesslike image. The grey flannel or pinstripe suit is a classic that has been acceptable for formal business wear since the turn of the century. Grey is a neutral shade that neither advances nor retreats and has an anonymity that makes it a natural for business apparel. Women, like their male business counterparts, have adopted grey because it is a handsome, versatile fashion color as well as a classic. Clothing should be a background for the talent and expertise of business people, and the grey suit has become almost the business uniform because it is so versatile yet inconspicuous.

Grey can be worn by both sunlights and moon glows, because it may have a warm undertone or a blue undertone. Soft pinks and blues combine well with grey to enhance a moon glow complexion. Burgundy and blued reds and purple are excellent accent colors. Sunlights can select a warm charcoal grey or a light grey with greenish undertones. These greys combine well with cream, ivory, and yellow and can be accented with red-orange accessories.

Fashion cycles affect the use of grey, especially in women's wear. Neutrals have longer cycles than bright fashion colors. Beige and grey are the two main neutral families, and generally the cycles for each last approximately 10 years. Often, these neutrals are popular in home furnishings, paints, and home and office accessories. During the 1980s, the grey family was the most fashionable neutral.

Grey, black, and white often are combined for a sophisticated color story. Wearing a dominant neutral story close to the face requires more dramatic rouge, lipstick, and eyeshadow so the complexion does not wash out. Color reflects on the face, and can make a subtle complexion look dull.

30

White

WHITE, TOO, IS TECHNICALLY a noncolor. When light containing all visible wavelengths falls on a surface with no pigment, all the wavelengths are reflected and the eye sees white.

White has many shades and personalities. White can seem pure and virginal (the classic wedding dress), cold and sterile, or neutral. Since it can reflect minute shades of other colors while still seeming white, it is a perfect neutral. The great variety of white tones offered in any paint store are designed to go with many different color types and tones of interior fabrics and wall coverings. Large expanses of pure white seem sterile and are usually tinted for interiors. Learn from this when selecting your apparel. White flatters the face because it reflects a pure light and provides a contrast to the warm shades of the complexion. White directs the eye to the face and highlights it. This characteristic, combined with the ability of white to work with almost the entire range of colors, makes it the most versatile neutral.

White is the classic men's shirt color. White is a power color only when combined with darks. The all-white "ice cream suit" has become the signature of author Tom Wolfe, who is also a very successful lecturer. He stands out in a crowd of neutral business suits, and the white suit is an appropriate way to highlight Mr. Wolfe's eclectic personality. An all-white sports outfit or casual outfit with white slacks looks very upper crust. It is typical of upper-class sports like tennis and yachting and has a crisp, well-kept look.

Sunlights and moon glows can both wear white, in one of its tinted versions, very successfully. Creamy, warm tones are best on the sunlight complexions. Ivory is the best white next to a sunlight's face. A slightly peachy undertone will flatter a yellow complexion. Blue-based whites and pure white are handsome on moon glows. A hint of pink also flatters the cool complexion.

White can seem frivolous and casual or elegant and dramatic for evening and formal wear. It is an excellent swimwear color in an opaque fabric, because it provides high contrast to a tan skin. White reflects heat and is the classic summertime color. Because white also reflects light, the parts of the body it covers will seem larger than with dark or neutral apparel.

31

Color Illusions

PROFESSIONAL APPAREL DESIGNERS use many color illusions to create special effects. Designing for a special figure requires constant attention to the way colors affect the body's proportions. When the consumer combines garments from several different manufacturers or selects pieces from a group of coordinated sportswear, he or she then becomes a stylist and should know the basic rules of color illusion that will enhance the particular figure type. Some of the most common color illusions that apply to apparel design follow. Most are as applicable to men as to women.

1. *Light values advance and make a thing seem larger; dark values recede and reduce.* It is important to remember this illusion, especially when combining colors in an outfit. Dark, subdued colors are used on a part of the body that the designer wishes to minimize. A woman with large hips and thighs and a small bust would dress to camouflage this problem in a dark pair of pants or a skirt and a light blouse. A dark top and a light bottom can be worn to camouflage a full bust.

This color illusion is the basis for dressing large women in black and somber colors. Unfortunately, though dark colors minimize bulk, they are often depressing and unflattering to the face. Deep, jewel tones, instead of black and somber colors, create the same illusion and are more flattering. To flatter the face, wear a light collar, or tie a bright scarf at the neck of a dark outfit.

A rugby shirt is an excellent example of a man's garment that uses light/dark contrast to emphasize the positive. A light or bright stripe at the chest creates the illusion of wide shoulders and chest, the desirable shape for the male physique. A rugby shirt often has a white collar, a design that directs attention to the face. The classic dark suit with a light shirt creates a V shape accent color emphasizing the shoulders and focusing attention on the neck. A suit tends to make a short man seem taller than a sports coat with a contrasting pant.

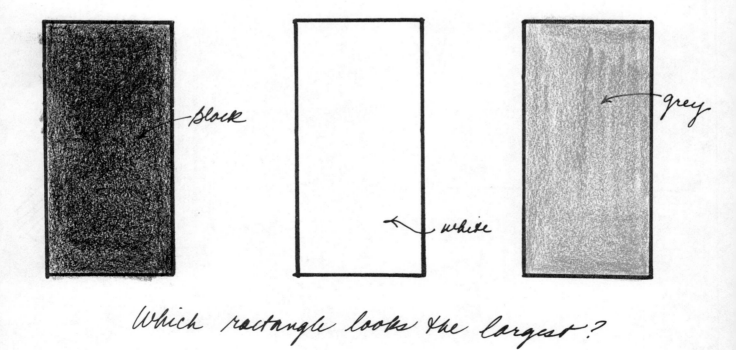

black

white

grey

Which rectangle looks the largest?

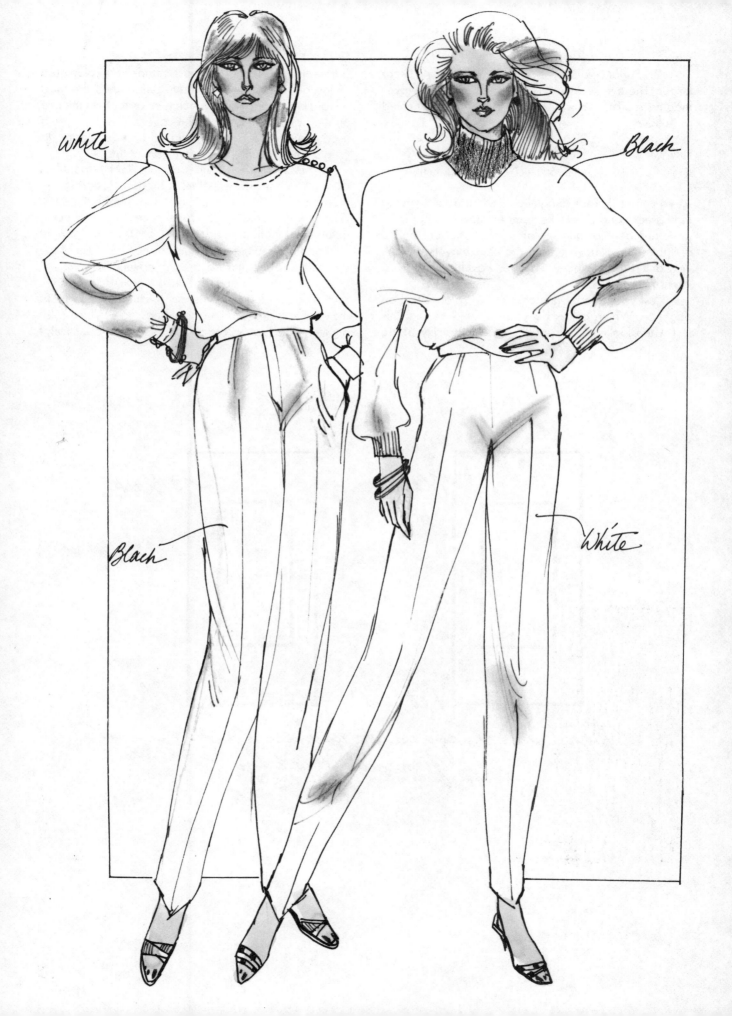

White

Black

Black

White

2. *Bright colors advance and make a thing seem larger.* The eye seeks out light with the longest wavelength first. The wavelengths of pure color are rated as follows:

Red: 700–600   Orange: 610–590   Yellow: 590–570

Green: 570–500   Blue: 500–460   Violet: 460–400

As you can see, reds and yellows are more advancing than greens and violets. Remember, these are approximate numbers for *pure* colors. Colors that are dulled or lightened will have greatly modified wavelengths. A very dull red could have a shorter wavelength than an intense turquoise.

Test your eye by glancing at the color wheel on page 27. Which colors do you see first? Repeat this test when looking at an outfit. Glance quickly at the garments, registering the most compelling color area of the outfit, and you will have determined the most advancing color. The advancing color focuses the eye on the part of the body that it covers. This principle is used repeatedly in every kind of apparel design to create interest and contrast in an outfit.

The classic man's suit is an excellent example. A dark suit contrasts with the light shirt, focusing the viewer's eye on the upper torso, and a bright tie is like an arrow that points to the face. A tie in an advancing color combination stands out in contrast to the light shirt and dark suit, gaining importance because of the contrast and the limited area it covers.

Color the squares in the example below as directed and evaluate the intensity of colors. Relate this to the garments illustrated on the facing page. Which color highlights the person's face and torso most effectively?

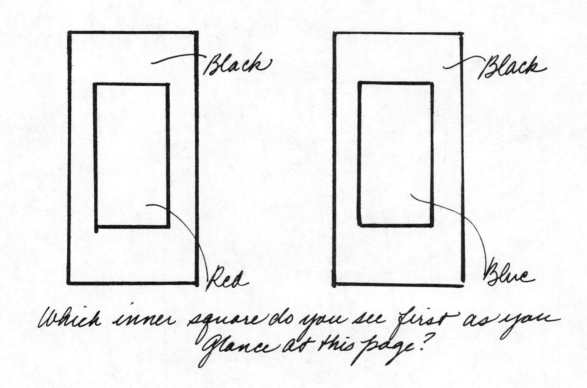

Black   *Black*

Red   *Blue*

Which inner square do you see first as you glance at this page?

Red and
Black

Cobalt
and
Black

Cobalt
Blue

Red

Which color
focuses your
attention on the
face first?

Which coat
did you notice
first?

Black

Black

3. *Light values placed near dark colors seem darker; dark values make light colors seem lighter.* This illusion of contrast is most important for judging the intensity of a color that is best suited for your complexion. A sunlight person with dark hair and a deep tan will make a light peach blouse or shirt seem pale. The light shade of the garment will make the dark skin tone seem darker than if the person was wearing a brown blouse or shirt. Dark velvet on a fair complexion will make the skin seem even lighter than it is. The person with a pale complexion has to balance a dark garment with more dramatic makeup or select a dark jewel

tone rather than black, dark brown, or charcoal to enhance the complexion.

Color the nearby boxes as indicated. Contrast is one of the most powerful visual elements in apparel design. Persons with high-contrast complexions usually can wear a wider range of colors than those with mono-tone complexions. Designers often use value contrast to avoid monotony and create interest, but this must be done with a delicate balance so the viewer is not overwhelmed. Too much contrast will create a confusing garment that "wears" the wearer, instead of enhancing their appearance.

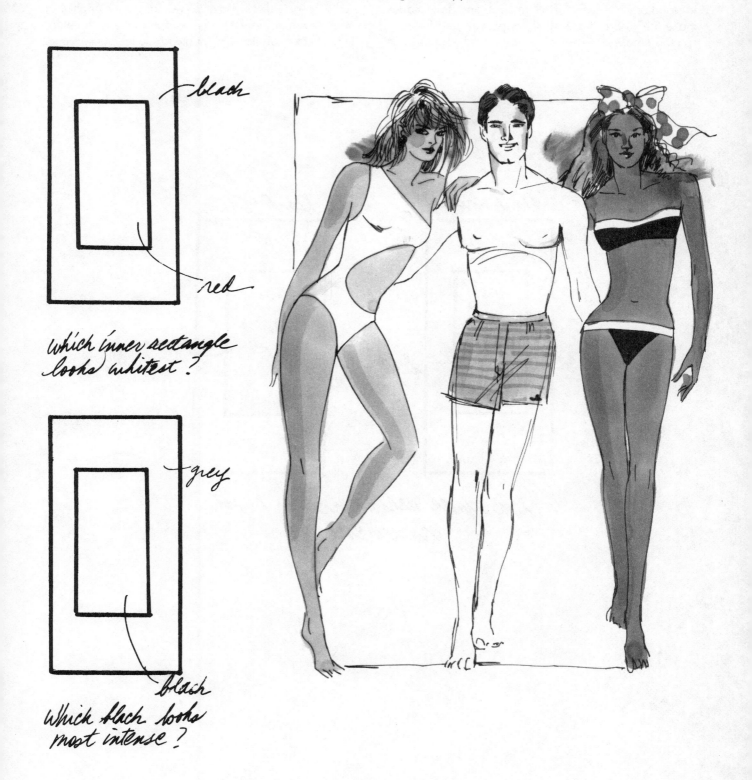

black

red

which inner rectangle looks whitest?

grey

black

which black looks most intense?

4. *Intensely colored clothing stands out against a duller background, making the wearer stand out. Neutral clothing against a neutral or more intense background makes the person less noticeable.* This illusion may be used to design uniforms, business clothing, and clothing for any individual who does not wish to stand out in a crowd. Dull, neutral, and dark shades make the wearer less visually apparent, and the person must make a verbal impact on his colleagues to be noticed. Picture how the classic waiter often blends into the surroundings, camouflaged by his apparel.

Again the boxes below illustrate the truth of this principle, which you can use to advantage if an occasion for which you are dressing is one in which it is appropriate to focus attention on yourself, then wear the red dress or jacket if you are a woman, or the bright tie if you are a man. Select clothing appropriate to the situation to make you stand out or blend into the background.

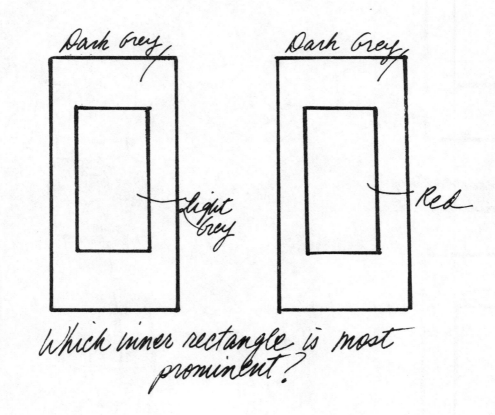

Dark Grey   *Light grey*   *Dark Grey*   *Red*

Which inner rectangle is most prominent?

Dark Grey

Silver

Red

Which dress focuses attention on wearer first?

5. *Large areas of dull colors are needed to balance small areas of bright colors.* This illusion is a logical result of illusion 2. Bright colors demand so much attention that they dominate large areas of dull color. Notice how coloring the blocks below proves this principle. Furthermore, large, unbroken areas of bright color are often too intense to view for long periods of time, for they create perception fatigue. The eye must have a resting place, a neutral area, so that the detail or accent color can become interesting and important—like the cinnamon and spice that makes the flour and milk tasty in a cake.

Apply this rule to dressing a person with low-intensity makeup and complexion in bright clothing. The intensity of the garment will overwhelm the low contrast complexion and dominate the visual personality of the wearer. Perhaps this principle exlains why inhabitants of tropical countries, whose complexions are typically tanned and who have dark hair, tend to prefer bright colors and brilliant white. A businessman in a dark suit with a white shirt and a red tie creates a strong color story that is handsome on a person with high-contrast coloring. A man with a more monochromatic complexion would look more attractive in a lighter suit, a blue shirt, and a subtle tie, because this combination would not dominate his complexion.

The same color principle is at work when assembling a woman's most flattering outfit. A woman with a pale skin and grey-brown hair would be dominated by a bright outfit. She would be more handsome in a subtle shading of flattering colors, with a bright accent to reflect positively on her neutral complexion.

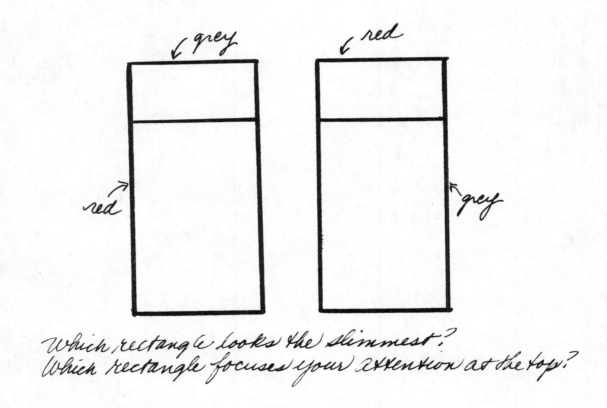

Which rectangle looks the slimmest?
Which rectangle focuses your attention at the top?

6. *An uninterrupted flow of color lengthens and slims a shape. A horizontal division of color shortens and adds width to a shape. Several different colors or values in an outift tend to make a figure seem shorter and wider, because the eye unconsciously compares the size and number of divisions and does not move as quickly as it would through a single-color composition.*

The three rectangles nearby demonstrate this illusion. Apply the principles to the garments pictured on the facing page. The interrupted flow of values and colors makes a person seem shorter than when wearing one solid color.

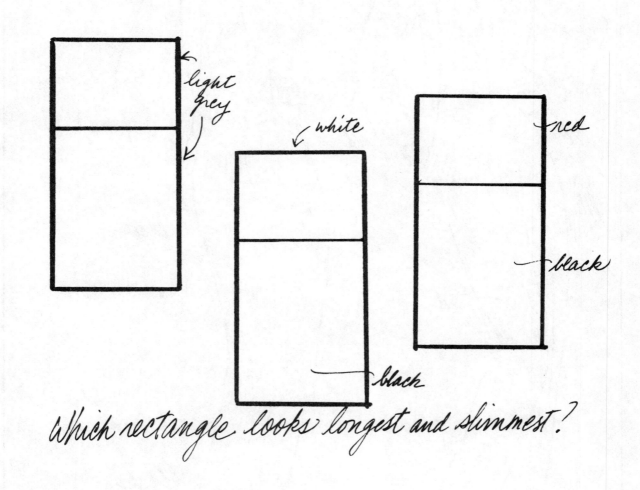

light grey

white

red

black

black

Which rectangle looks longest and slimmest?

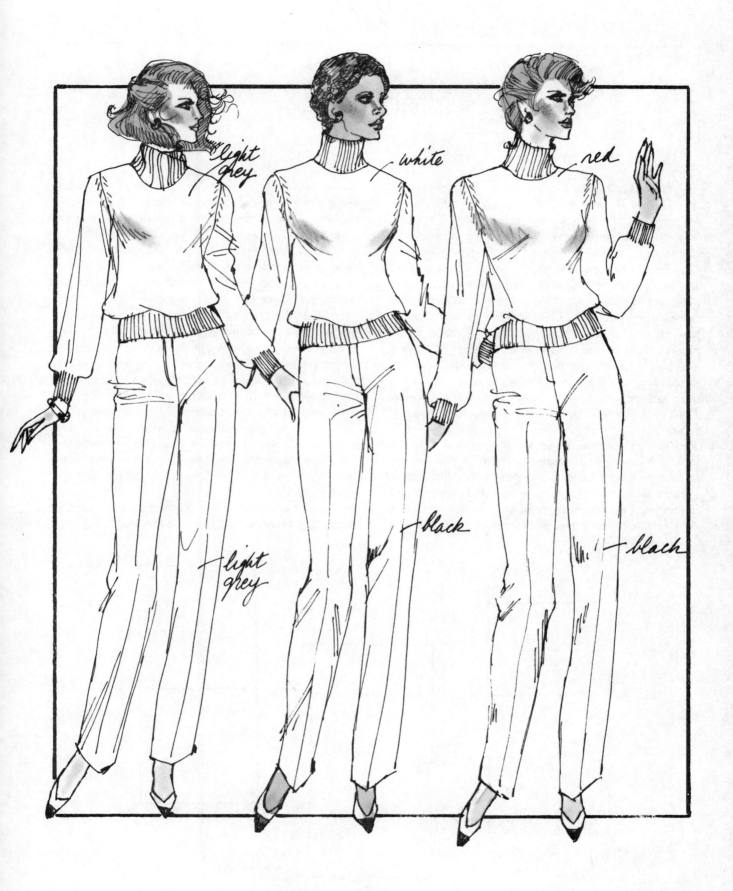

light
grey

white

red

black

light
grey

black

32

Proportion

*P*ROPORTION IS ONE of the factors that most influences the way an outfit looks. Proportion is the relationship of the size of the different parts of an outfit to one another and the relationship of the total volume of the garments to the figure wearing it.

People are accustomed to human proportions. The first rectangle below represents a woman's garment with a natural waistline and a skirt that falls two inches below the knee. Our "eye" reads this proportion as typical. A woman wearing a dress with this natural division would appear to a viewer to be her true height (unless she has a very short or very long torso). The same person wearing a garment with a modified proportion will appear to be taller or shorter. The eye is "fooled" by the illusion created by the different parts of the garments.

Evaluate the rectangles on this page. Which one looks the longest? which the shortest? The reason the middle rectangle looks the longest is that the viewer sees the bottom as a large, uninterrupted expanse and automatically compares it to the smaller top. This alteration of the expected proportions makes the

viewer see the figure as taller than the normal waistline garment. The tallest illusion is created by wearing a garment with no horizontal divisions, such as a shift or unbelted jumpsuit.

These rectangles illustrate the most important thing to remember about proportion: Horizontal divisions of a space that are similar in size shorten and widen the visual size of the space.

Study the dresses on the facing page, which further illustrate the same principle. Notice how the horizontal divisions of space at the natural waist or hip or under the bust make a remarkable difference in how tall and slender the figure looks. The figure on the right looks the shortest and thickest because the body is divided into two approximately equal spaces. It is an example of the unfortunate proportion of many two-piece maternity dresses. The already-wider figure of an expectant mother is made to seem fatter and shorter when she wears a garment that just covers her tummy.

Color emphasizes the parts of an outfit and the proportion of the total figure. Use tones of black, grey,

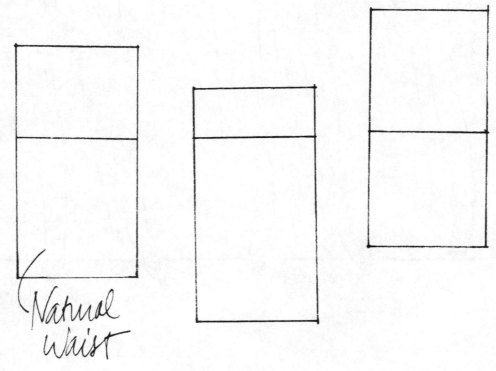

Natural waist

Natural Waist

Empire

Low Torso

and white to experiment with color-emphasized proportion. Make three copies of the natural-waist rectangle. Color one a solid grey, another with a white top and a black bottom, and the third with a black top and a white bottom. Notice how much longer the solid grey rectangle looks. Next compare the illusion of height created by the dark bottom and the light top. This rectangle seems the next longest, because the dark tone of the skirt tends to draw the eye downward and give weight to the larger space. The third example seems the shortest. The dark top compresses the smaller space and seems to depress the white area.

Menswear is visually evaluated in the same way. The natural waistline usually dominates the pants and shirt combination. Men who have a long torso and short legs or a short torso and long legs can use the color-emphasized rule of proportion to balance out their outfits. Men with short legs should carefully fit the length of their jacket so the proportion seems natural. To give the illusion of longer legs, wear the same tone in tops and bottoms or dark bottoms with a lighter top.

33

Proportion Illusions

*T*HE HIGH-FASHION DESIGNER modifies proportion each season, creating garments that emphasize or exaggerate a part of the body to create a specific fashion illusion. Ordinarily, designers use proportion to make women seem taller and thinner. This is the current ideal of beauty. The rules that create this illusion can be reversed to shorten the very tall person. A theatrical costume designer may play with proportion to make a character in a movie or play seem dumpier or fatter than the person really is. The rules of proportion are not good or bad; they are devices to emphasize parts of the body to create a specific look.

The dresses on the previous pages are simple examples of the effect of horizontal divisions. There are many possible variations on this idea relating to basic silhouettes of outfits, color counterbalances, and so forth. For example, reversing the large and small spaces in a garment will also create an illusion of height. The drop torso is an excellent way to visually lengthen the upper torso of a short-waisted person, an illusion that may balance the tendency of a lowered waist to reduce overall height. The drop torso dress will draw attention to the hips, which are often larger than the top, so only a person with a slim hip can wear this silhouette, but layering will allow other figure proportions to wear this silhouette. A vest, overtop, or jacket that covers the hip line, especially including any bulges or extra weight, will slim the figure when worn with a straight or tapered pant leg. The layered garment balances the wider hip line and the smaller bust of a pear-shaped figure, and creates an illusion of height, especially when the top is the same color as the bottom.

A very short skirt also makes a person seem taller. This silhouette, especially the simple flared garment first made popular in the 1960s by André Corregges, has a youthful look. Slender, well-shaped legs are essential to its success. The relatively short expanse of dress contrasted with the visible length of leg makes the wearer seem taller. Dark hose and shoes emphasize the effect. Skin-tone shoes and natural stockings, or shoes the same color as the stockings, make anyone seem taller. A contrasting shoe pulls the viewer's atten-

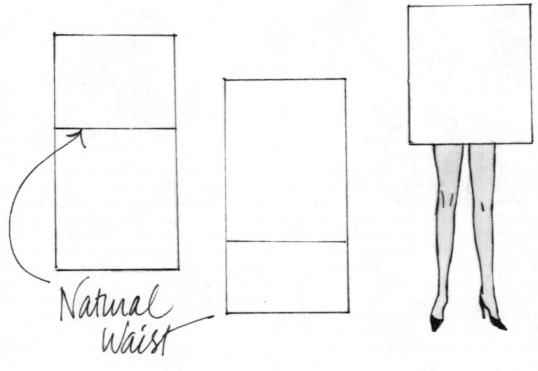

Natural waist

tion downward and detracts from the impact of the garment's proportion. Feet look larger in a contrasting shoe.

Color tone and intensity emphasize and dramatize the elements of proportion. Dark, rich colors on the bottom tend to anchor the garment to the floor. A white or light top quickly leads the eye to the shoulders, neck, and face. Garments with no color contrast create a subtle illusion of height; a soft, neutral, or dark color has a greater elongating effect than a bright color.

Make copies of the nearby low torso and miniskirt rectangles, and experiment with color value relationships as you did in the last chapter. Compare the illusion created when the legs and shoes contrast or blend with the miniskirt example. Make copies of the garment examples shown above and try other combinations of light and dark. Experiment to see how color values work in combination with the proportion of the garment. Evaluate how effectively these combinations create the illusion of height.

34

Pants Proportion

*F*ASHION DESIGNERS use a wide variety of shapes and lengths to achieve particular effects when designing pants. Length determines the proportion of most pants. The illusion of height is created when the pant is long enough to cover a shoe with a medium to high heel. The long pant with a crisp front crease forms an unbroken vertical line from the waist downward, increasing the illusion of height. Pants fit is very important. Tight pants that cling to hip or stomach will bulge and show horizontal tension lines that emphasize the width of the body and detract from the illusion of length. A straight or slightly flared pant leg creates the longest leg line.

The shape, fullness, and details of men's and women's pants are determined by popular fashion of the day. The eye gradually adjusts to new silhouettes, which often evolve in fashion cycles that take many years. Styling details change from season to season.

The two main pants categories for both men and women are jeans and trousers. Though made from different kinds of fabrics and though fitting differently, the principles of proportion and the vertical emphasis are the same in both. Jeans are made from heavyweight denim that is sturdily stitched and riveted so it can fit tightly over the waist and stomach. Trousers are usually made from fabrics like gabardine, flannel, poplin, or sheeting. Trousers cannot fit as tightly as jeans, because the seams are not reinforced and the fabrics often are not as strong as denim or lack denim's natural elasticity (called *recovery*). The trouser should fit smoothly, with some ease, over the hips and stomach and fall in a smooth line from the fullest part of the torso to the floor. Some women can wear men's jeans, which fit low on the hip, making a good line for a woman with a straight torso. The classic female figure—small waist and rounded hips—does not fit in men's pants easily.

Pants length for men is not an important fashion issue. Most dress pants cover the shoe and taper slightly at the heel. Men wearing shorts select length for comfort and practicality. A much greater variety of lengths often are fashionable for women's pants. Wearing fashion lengths should be carefully calculated for the woman with the less-than-perfect figure.

Pants that end at the lower calf (the pedal pusher) will make the wearer seem shorter, even if worn with matching hose and shoes. Fuller pants, like the bloomer and the jodhpur, make the hips seem wider, because of the contrast of full hip with slim leg.

Shorts also will drastically affect the illusion of length. Short shorts worn by a person with long, slim legs and heeled shoes will have much the same effect as a miniskirt. Shorts add to the illusion of height, because the leg length becomes the dominant area of the silhouette. Pants that end at the top of the knee (the classic bermuda) can shorten the figure, especially when teamed with over-the-calf socks and casual low-heeled shoes. Many horizontal divisions of the leg shorten the figure.

grey

Royal
Blue

Dark
Grey

Royal
Blue

Grey

Violet,
Aqua
and
Royal
Blue

Pink

Lavender

White

Chocolate

35

Horizontal Proportions

A PRIMARY RULE OF PROPORTION says that the viewer's eye automatically compares the larger portion of a divided space with the smaller area. A small area appears even smaller when surrounded by larger spaces. Which white square below looks narrower? ·The effect of the silhouette of a garment depends on this automatic comparison of volumes. By exaggerating one horizontal area of an outfit, the other parts of the body can be minimized.

Visual perception of clothing also compares the volume of fabric to the actual size of the figure underneath. "Tricking" the eye to read size as having been created by fabric rather than by an excess of flesh is the primary goal of a designer. A person can camouflage a figure problem by balancing the volume, color, and shape of a garment to create the illusion of a slender body. The extremely thin person can make use of the same balancing tricks to make the body seem less angular. Designers often experiment with oversized garments, because large clothes, properly fit and proportioned, can create the illusion of a slim body under the clothes.

Women's fashions have greater silhouette variation than menswear. There are four basic dress silhouettes: the hourglass, the rectangle, the wedge, and the flared silhouette. The hourglass silhouette makes the waist seem smaller because the hip and bust or shoulders are emphasized. Volume might be added to the hips with a full skirt and to the upper torso with full, puffy sleeves. A small waist is a desirable feminine characteristic.

The rectangle silhouette bypasses the waist and emphasizes height. This silhouette camouflages a thick waist and is less feminine.

The wedge-shaped silhouette contrasts a widened shoulder line with a narrow hip. This is the ideal masculine silhouette, and men's business suits and jackets are cut and padded to reinforce it. The wedge silhouette is popular for women during periods when assertive feminine roles are desirable in society. The wedge shape tends to add height, especially if the shoulder extension is not too extreme. When worn by women, pants and long skirts also emphasize height.

The flared silhouette is a natural, comfortable shape for women that adds to height and makes the hips and waist seem slim. The flared skirt also seems to slim the leg, by contrasting it with the full volume of the skirt.

Garments that fit poorly destroy the intended illusion of a design. A garment that is skimpy or too tight does not elongate the figure. The horizontal wrinkle

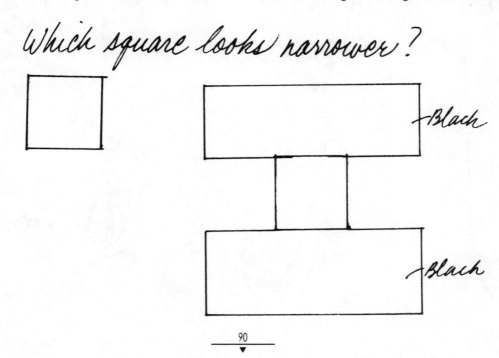

Which square looks narrower?

Black

Black

Hourglass

Wedge

Flared

lines that are the inevitable result of too small a garment carry the eye across the figure, emphasizing width and not height or slimness. A garment that is too large may make the wearer seem bulkier.

Fashion decrees the silhouette and proportion popular during a fashion cycle. The public's eye gradually becomes accustomed to a new proportion, which becomes more normal as it is interpreted from radical high fashion to wearable street fashion. The wise dresser follows the fashion trends, but interprets them as evolution rather than revolution. Adopt the best silhouettes and details that flatter your figure. Avoid fashions that are too radical or unflattering. Analyze your figure type, and experiment with garments that draw attention to the best parts of your body.

36

Line

*L*INE REFERS TO THE EDGE or outline of a garment and the style lines that divide the space within a garment. Line creates visual effects because it leads the eye. Artfully used, line can make the body look taller and slimmer.

Vertical style lines emphasize height because they lead the eye up and down the garment, with less attention being focused on the width of the figure. Horizontal style lines emphasize width, again because the line leads the eye. Diagonal style lines often have a slimming effect. Curved lines are feminine and passive. Curved style lines are used at necklines and in collars, ruffles, and other design details in women's wear. Rounded collars and ruffles are youthful. The more exaggerated a curved line is, the more time it takes to view the contour.

Study the optical illusions created by the linear diagrams on this page. The way the lines are arranged determines how long they seem, although all the verticals are the same length. The third example from the left looks the shortest because the eye is distracted from the vertical with diagonal downward lines. The fourth example falls between the extremes. The vertical line is a focal point, and the abrupt horizontals give the figure a strong, compact look.

These abstract examples illustrate the illusions that can be created by garments. The first example translates into the dress with the V neckline. The central vertical and two diagonals create a slimming and lengthening line. This illusion is enhanced if the V is emphasized by a contrasting blouse with a dark jacket. Analyze a man's suit and notice the V line, emphasized by the diagonals of the lapel and the vertical tie. Worn with sharply creased pants, these elements emphasize the vertical. Men's jackets are padded at the shoulder to emphasize the shoulder line (or create a wedge shape).

The diagonal line in the second garment slims the figure more than horizontal style lines would, but it makes the figure seem shorter than the first example. The dress that has strong horizontal style lines makes the person look wider at the shoulder and balances a wide hip. A single, strong vertical style line makes a person seem tall and slender, especially when there is no waist definition.

Very tall women who wish to look shorter should use lines that break a strong vertical. Contrasting layers of clothing—such as jackets, sweaters, and vests—add horizontal divisions. Bold accessories such as contrast belts, bold jewelry, and mixtures of textures and colors make a person seem shorter.

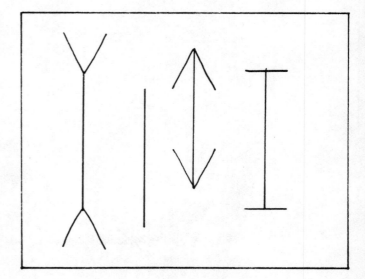

37

Vertical Style Lines

*M*ORE THAN ONE vertical line in a garment divides the area so the eye reads the combined spaces as smaller than the whole. To confirm this statement, decide which of the three rectangles at the bottom of the page looks the slimmest and tallest.

One type of vertical division in a garment is called a *gore.* Gores are separate pieces of shaped fabric that form a garment when sewn together. Because gores form an unbroken line along the length of a garment, they make the wearer seem slimmer and taller. Darts also form vertical divisions. They shape the fabric to the figure, but they do not connect the edges of the garment. Because they are not continuous, they "drop" the eye as it looks at the garment. The shorter, broken line of a dart makes a person seem shorter than would a garment with a continuous vertical style line.

The garments on the facing page translate the illusions illustrated in the abstract rectangles to actual garments. Evaluate the garments before you color them in, to see the impact of style line only. Then color

the garment as indicated. The first dress is called a float, chemise, or shift. This dress has a boxy fit, with no waist definition. A tall, slender person wearing this style seems even taller. The float can also camouflage a thick waist and balance a heavy bust. Color the dress a light tone, and evaluate it with the other two garments. Take a narrow marking pen and draw in a vertical stripe pattern. Notice how the addition of stripes emphasizes the vertical space and makes the dress seem longer and more slender than when plain. Narrow stripes are most effective; wider stripes look very busy.

The single center front seam is a long, slenderizing line. This effect can be exaggerated by color. A dramatic color difference between the two sides of the dress, half white and half black, for example, divides the space so the viewer sees two spaces smaller than the whole. Experiment with the optical illusions possible with two colors. On a tracing of the dress, color one side bright red and the other white. Notice how

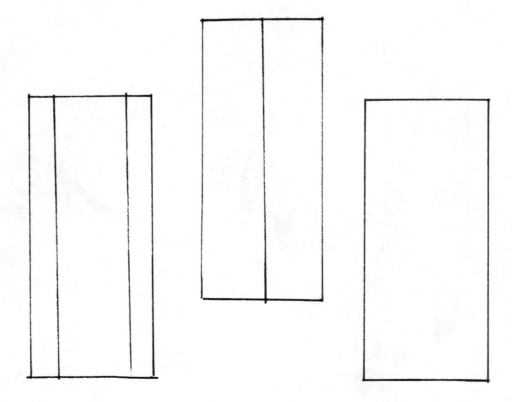

confusing this color combination is. Both red and white are advancing colors. The two used together visually enlarge the space instead of making it smaller. The secret of the slenderizing two-color trick is to make half the dress recede while the other advances.

The final example is the princess line, also a slimming garment. The vertical lines are created by large gores starting from the armhole or shoulder. The figure seems taller and slimmer because the space is broken up into smaller vertical divisions. Now copy the dress on tracing paper, and color the center panel black and the two sides white. How does the change alter the illusion of the garment? Too many vertical divisions dilute the effect, and the garment will look confused because it lacks a clean styling theme. The busier a garment is, the more difficult it becomes for the average figure to wear. The tall, slender woman can wear a much more complicated garment than a shorter person with a bulkier figure.

Chemise

Shift

Gored Princess Line

38

Horizontal Style Lines

HORIZONTAL LINES EMPHASIZE the width of the figure. Carefully used, they are very effective styling devices. Horizontal lines can attract the viewer's attention to a part of the body that should be emphasized to balance another part. Horizontal style lines often are used in men's sportswear to emphasize a broad chest. A sweater with a horizontal design at the chest is a classic example.

Narrow shoulders can be widened visually by a strong horizontal, such as a shoulder yoke. Soft gathers coming from a shoulder yoke add the feminine effect of curved lines and control the additional fabric needed over the bust.

A small waist, highlighted with a bright belt, seems even smaller if contrasted with a full blouse and skirt—the rule of contrasting proportion and horizontal design lines. The wider the belt, the more the area will be emphasized. A simple seam or narrow, self-colored belt attracts the least attention. No contrast at the waistline slims a thick waist. A horizontal division at the waist is a natural proportion for both men and women.

Horizontal style lines are used in combination with vertical darts to fit a woman's garment. For example, the waistline seam controls the ease needed to allow the garment to fit the wider hips and bust. Horizontal style lines can be decorative as well as functional when used to inset a contrast color or fabric in a garment.

Carefully used horizontal stripes correct some figure problems. Balance a large hip line and a small torso with a horizontal striped top. Border prints or details such as tucks at the hemline shorten a woman who is very tall, because they pull the eye down to the design.

Drop torso garments visually widen the hip line and are most effectively worn by tall, slender women. Contrasting belts and style lines at the hip balance a large bust by making the hips seem wider.

Evaluate the rectangles at the bottom of the page. Notice how the vertical and horizontal lines work together to create many different illusions and how they translate into garments.

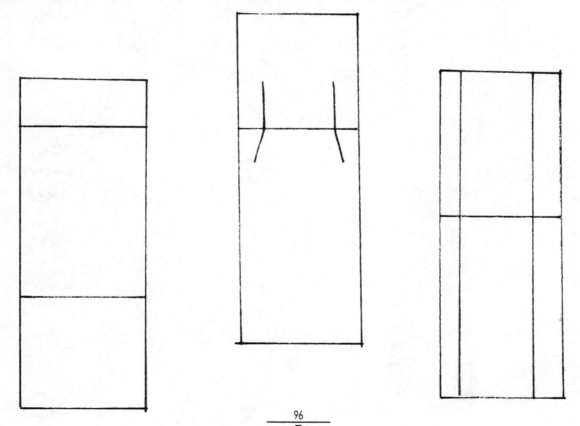

39

The Most Important Horizontal—
The Hemline

THE MOST IMPORTANT HORIZONTAL style line in a skirted garment is the hem. The length of the skirt influences the entire proportion and all the other style elements of the garment. Hemlines are dictated by fashion. Public acceptance of a radical hemline change and new proportion takes time. The customer must get used to the new proportion and experiment with it. A skirt that does not conform to current fashion will look dated, but there is usually a range of acceptable lengths. The trick is to determine the most flattering length for you from the currently acceptable fashions.

Experiment to determine which skirt length is most flattering before you go shopping. Your attention is often distracted in a clothing store. Many people concentrate on the color or the style or the price of the garment without evaluating its total proportion in relation to their own figure type—and that is the most important element in selecting a successful garment.

To experiment with skirt length, you must have a full-length mirror. Assemble the following materials:

▼ A leotard or similar simple top
▼ A piece of dark fabric, wide enough to wrap around you and long enough to cover you from the waist to the floor
▼ A variety of stockings—skin tone, dark, and light
▼ A sampling of your shoe wardrobe, including flats, medium heels, high heels, and boots
▼ A variety of belts—wide and narrow, dark and bright; also a piece of half-inch elastic tied into a circle the size of your waist

Wearing the leotard, wrap the fabric around your body like a skirt and secure it with the elastic. Start by wearing skin-tone hose and flat shoes. Adjust the "skirt" to several lengths. Evaluate the effect created by the hem length in relation to your figure until you have found the most flattering length. Go through the same procedure with different stockings and shoes in different combinations. Experiment with the belts. Notice how a contrasting belt more clearly

defines the length of the skirt and may require a slightly longer hemline to create the illusion of height. A general rule for slimming the leg is to end the hem at the fullest curve of the leg so only a tapering column is visible.

Experimenting with skirt lengths at home before you go shopping allows you to adapt current fashion trends to a length that is flattering to your figure. You may have to repeat the hemline experiment to evaluate a new fashion length, but you can train your eye to see the best hem length.

A flattering leg line is created when the hem stops below the fullest part of the leg's curve. This applies to above-the-knee lengths as well as below-the-knee. Dark hose will camouflage ugly knees when fashion demands shorter shirts.

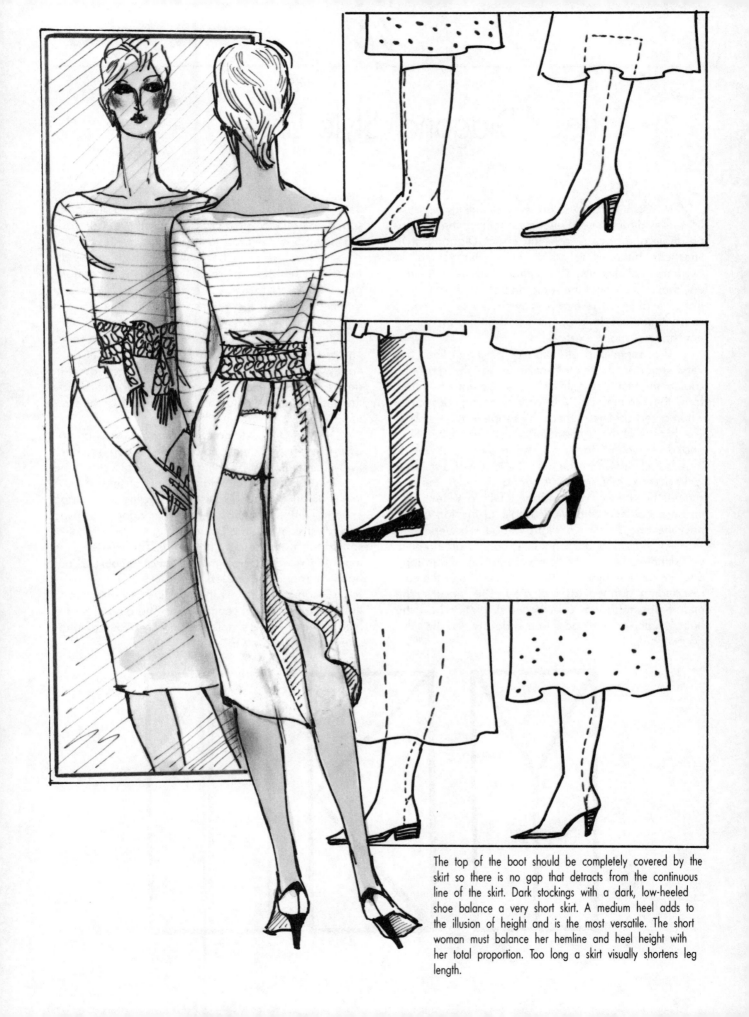

The top of the boot should be completely covered by the skirt so there is no gap that detracts from the continuous line of the skirt. Dark stockings with a dark, low-heeled shoe balance a very short skirt. A medium heel adds to the illusion of height and is the most versatile. The short woman must balance her hemline and heel height with her total proportion. Too long a skirt visually shortens leg length.

40

Diagonal Style Lines

*D*IAGONAL STYLE LINES are very slimming, because they direct the eye over the curves of the body at an angle and have a softening effect. Diagonal style lines can be used to create either symmetrical or asymmetrical designs. The human body is symmetrical; that is, it is about the same on both sides of a central vertical line. The eye sees symmetry as the norm, so asymmetrical designs, in which the sides are different, have a more exotic look.

The angle and direction of diagonal lines are very important to the effectiveness of the garment. Look at the first rectangle below. As we have seen before, the symmetrical V is very slimming, especially when a vertical line extends the shape to the hemline. The face is at the focal point of the V neckline. Shirt and dress collars form this shape when left unbuttoned. Jackets worn open and the lapels of a tailored jacket create a V shape. A strong shoulder line is a successful way to style a garment with a V neck, because it balances the wider angle at the top of the neckline and creates a slight wedge silhouette.

Asymmetrical diagonal lines can be an effective and slimming way to style a garment. Notice how long and slender the middle rectangle looks. Color the corresponding garment as indicated. The black in the midriff deemphasizes a bulky waist. Notice how the floor-length gown adds tremendously to the illusion of height.

The final example uses the arrowhead division of space naturally created by a raglan sleeve. Contrasting the body of the dress to the sleeves creates greater emphasis on the arrowhead shape, which draws attention on the face. The raglan sleeve is very comfortable and tends to make the wearer look taller and slimmer, because the seams direct the eye upward and diagonally across the body. Raglans are very popular for men's casual jackets and knit sports shirts. The less structured shoulder line is easier to fit on a variety of shoulder shapes and widths than a set-in sleeve. The angle of the sleeve line is determined by the designer and should not be too radical, or the slimming effect is lost.

Asymmetrical diagonal lines can correct an unbalanced figure. A high hip or shoulder can be effectively camouflaged by using a diagonal to direct the eye away from the unbalanced part of the body. A low shoulder can be disguised by leaving it bare and covering the higher shoulder with a diagonal neckline and fitted sleeve. On a balanced figure, the diagonal should run from the right to the left. The Western eye tends to follow a design in that format because of our habit of reading from left to right.

Diagonal lines over the bust line call attention to the bust and make it seem larger. The diagonal of a high V neckline or a simple raglan will not overemphasize the bust, however.

41

Curved Lines

CURVED LINES are feminine. The gentle curve of a jewel neckline compliments a woman's natural body shape. A deep, curved neckline emphasizes the roundness of the bust and shoulders and has a sensuous, feminine look.

The most exaggerated curved line in apparel design, the ruffle, has always been a symbol of femininity. The ruffle softens style lines and is romantic and fragile looking. The curved line of a ruffle holds the eye longer than a straight line, making the ruffle the focal point of a garment. The eye passes quickly over the smooth parts of a dress to focus on the ruffle. A face is highlighted by a ruffled neckline, the hands by a frill at the wrist. A large, full ruffle is the most exaggerated curved line. It takes more time to look at this shape, so a ruffled garment can look too busy unless carefully designed.

The direction of a curve creates a specific illusion. The hem of a garment that has a downward curve across the stomach makes the stomach seem rounder. A blouse or sweater worn over pants or a skirt should be arranged with an upward curve over the stomach. This line is more slimming, because it directs the eye upward and deemphasizes a round stomach. A slight, even, downward-curved hemline of a full, flared skirt flatters the legs. An upward curve at the front of a skirt makes the bust or stomach look as if it is protruding and distorting the skirt. A jacket should be slightly longer in the back, creating a slight diagonal when viewed from the side, which slims the hip line.

Curved style lines, ruffles, soft bows, and other such details make a woman seem more feminine. Because these details tend to be "fussy" and make for a more visually complicated garment, they make a person seem shorter. But a blouse with controlled ruffles worn with a tailored suit softens the appearance of the wearer without detracting from the businesslike image the suit imparts. A tall, angular woman can use these softening style devices very effectively. The shorter woman with a full figure emphasizes her bulges if she overdoes the use of curved lines in an outfit. She can wear bows and ruffles, but they should be smaller and more controlled.

Curved silhouette lines camouflage the too-slim and the too-plump figure if they are not overdone. The eye reads the soft, curved fabric bloused into a belt line as a part of the garment and not as flesh. On the facing page, notice how the garment on the right uses soft, curved lines to camouflage bulges at the waist. Slight fullness does not distract from the vertical line and slims the figure. Puffy, full, curved lines emphasize roundness and make a full figure seem fat.

The same principles apply to hairstyles. A round hair style emphasizes the roundness of a face, while soft, vertical curves detract from the roundness. Reverse the rule if you are softening a long face or an angular jawline. The softness of a rounded hairstyle makes the long face seem more feminine and shorter.

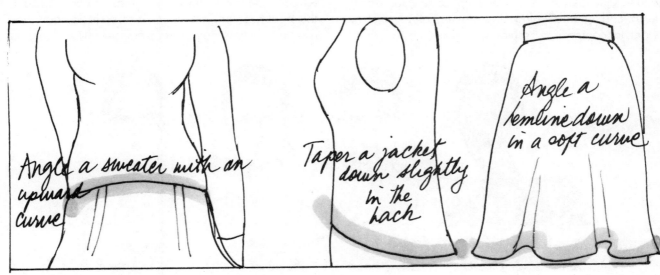

42

Face, Neck, and Shoulder Shapes: Women

*T*HE PERSONALITY AND APPEARANCE of the face, neck, and shoulders can be greatly changed by illusions created by the shape of a neckline and hairstyle. There are four basic face shapes: oval, square, round, and triangular. Let us review the effects of line and then apply them to face, neck, and shoulder shapes.

- ▼ Horizontal lines broaden and shorten.
- ▼ Vertical lines slim and elongate.
- ▼ Diagonal lines slim and elongate.
- ▼ Curved lines are feminine, and emphasize roundness and softness.

Look at your face, neck, and shoulders in a mirror. Compare your face shape, shoulder shape, and neck length with the illustrations below. The fashion ideal is a slim, oval face with a medium-to-long neck and a well-defined shoulder line. This has not always been the fashion ideal. During the 1890s, rounded, sloping shoulders and a round face were considered most beautiful. During the flapper era, narrow shoulders and a thin, pointed face were preferred. During the 1950s, fashion models had small, neat shoulders and oval faces. During each period, most women can achieve the ideal of beauty by emphasizing some features and camouflaging or softening others if they want to conform to fashion's standards.

The shape and line of a hairstyle can modify face shape. Work with a talented hairstylist to find an appropriate style for you. Clip examples of hairstyles you like from magazines, and spend some time talking to the stylist before your hair is washed and cut. Try parting your hair in different places. Analyze the direction your hair grows and its fullness. Consider the effect of different styles on the shape of your face. If your face is too round, do not select a round, full style that will make it seem rounder; choose an asymmetrical style with some soft vertical curves. A triangular face can be balanced by fullness at the chin line; soft waves just above the shoulder will accomplish this. Fullness at the temples diminishes the impact of a square jaw. Oval faces can wear a great diversity of hairstyles successfully.

Consider your life-style before selecting a hairstyle. Nothing is less attractive than hair that is unbrushed, dirty, and unattractively cut. You can wash your hair as often as you like if you make sure to rinse out all the soap each time you shampoo. Hair can be easily dried and styled attractively when it is cut to conform to its natural growth patterns. The length and type of cut will give the head the most attractive shape and volume to compliment the face and figure. If your schedule does not allow you to make frequent trips to the beauty salon, ask your hairdresser to show you how to style your hair. Everyone should have their hair

Ideal–Oval
medium to long neck

Round Face
short neck

Square Jaw
thick neck

Triangle
long neck.

trimmed every four to six weeks, even if letting the hair grow. Careful shaping allows the hair to grow and not look awkward when in transition from one style to another.

Next, work with necklines to discover the lines that enhance your face and neck. Sit in front of a mirror. Use the same fabric you used for the skirt experiment. Drape the fabric around your shoulders to form the neckline shapes drawn below. Experiment with necklaces of different shapes over the dark drape. Short necklaces and chokers make the face seem rounder and fuller at the chin line. They also shorten the visual length of the neck. The deep curve of an opera-length necklace (24 to 28 inches) creates an illusion of height. Its almost vertical lines

lengthen a round face and make the neck seem longer and more slender. The size of your bust will dictate the length of the necklace that is most flattering. A woman with a large bust should avoid necklaces that call attention to her chest. Select a shorter style with no dangling ornaments that fall on the bosom. Notice how you can combine two effects, for example, broadening the shoulders with a bateau neckline and lengthening the neck and face with a V-shaped chain and pendant.

As you experiment, note the successful lines. Try on several of your favorite blouses and compare them to the experiments you have made. Study this information so you have a specific idea, before you go shopping, of which necklines are the most flattering.

necklace can add illusion of longer neck

Boat or Bateau neck- Broadens shoulder line- shortens neck

Jewel neck- shortens neck, rounds face

Scoop neck- rounds face, body- slims neck

Lengthens face, neck

Emphasizes square jaw

Broadens shoulders

V-neck - lengthens face, slims neck

Slims face, neck

Turtleneck- modified can make neck look longer...... exaggerated makes neck shorter, face rounder

Shortens neck, rounds, softens face

Slims shoulders- corrects unbalanced shoulder

43

Face, Neck, and Shoulder Shapes: Men

MEN'S FACES COME IN THE same basic shapes as women's: oval, square, round, and triangular. While there is less fashion pressure on men to modify their facial silhouette, men with full faces often want to look slimmer. The fit and shape of the collar on a business shirt can make a man's face seem thinner. The fit and size of the collar will also camouflage a full or aging neck. Additionally, when a collar fits too snugly, it actually makes the neck look fat and is very uncomfortable. In business attire, the fit of the shirt collar is critical to a successful look, because the focus of a suit is on the neck and face. The large expanse of dark suit fabric leads the eye to the contrasting shirt front. The tie provides a dark or bright accent line that centers on the collar and face. Because a businessman's apparel focuses on the face, most people give the whole body a "once over" glance and view the man the same way a photographer would shoot a portrait.

Here is how to select the correct shirt collar size: The collar should fit comfortably, with enough room to slip the index finger inside the collar and run it around the front of the neck without having the collar bind. The collar should not cause the flesh of the neck to bulge when buttoned. Neither should the collar gap visibly at the side of the neck, which would make the neck look too skinny. Necks with a great deal of extra flesh, typical as a person ages, can be camouflaged by wearing a collar that is higher in the front and loose enough to allow a comfortable fit. Factory-made shirts are constructed with a variety of neck sizes and sleeve lengths, but may not fit a man whose shoulders or body do not conform to the average. Usually, such a man compromises, purchasing a collar size that is too small so the shirt fits his shoulders and body. The answer for this type of body is a custom-made shirt.

The shape of the collar should compliment the shape of the face. A wide, full face will look best in a standard collar worn with a tie with a large knot. Too small a collar and tie on a full face or a large man accentuates the size of the face. Avoid collar pins, and select a slightly longer point to the collar to emphasize vertical style lines.

A very thin face will be widened by a full spread collar and collars in contrasting colors. Beware, however, because contrasting collars are less formal, can be considered "trendy," and may be inappropriate for serious business. Wear a medium-size tie knot. A button-down collar that does not have long points also flatters this type of face.

A average-width face can wear a variety of collar shapes. The classic button-down has a conservative, slightly less formal business look. The standard

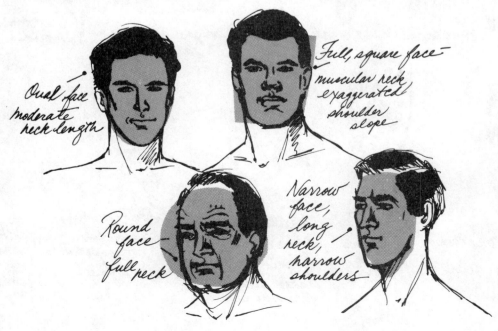

Oval face, moderate neck length

Full, square face, muscular neck, exaggerated shoulder slope

Round face, full neck

Narrow face, long neck, narrow shoulders

Too Tight | Correct Fit | Too Loose

Full Face
full knot
slightly longer points

Thin Face
moderate to wide spread
medium knot

Oval Face
medium neck
Great range of collar styles and spreads

Square Jaw
Wide spread with slightly longer points
full knot

collar, with average-length points, has a versatile look for both casual and serious business suits. Add a collar pin for a sophisticated, urban look. Novelty collars, such as contrasting colors and rounded points or other fashion-dictated shapes, should be selected for their appropriateness for the occasion and the outfit. The average face may wear a variety of knot sizes.

A few words about the bow tie. This is a marvelous novelty that makes a thin or angular face seem broader and more balanced. The bow tie should be avoided, however, if you have a very long or short neck. A bow tie is worn by a special kind of man. He must have a unique personality to carry it off and not look like Orville Redenbacker, the popcorn king! Although the bow tie is not taken as seriously as a con-

ventional tie for formal business wear, many very successful men have made it their signature. If you feel the bow tie is for you, or when worn for formal wear, learn how to tie the bow properly and avoid unattractive shortcuts like the clip-on or pretied band.

Shoulder shape is another key element in shirt fit. The shoulder yoke of a man's shirt should fit smoothly, without wrinkles at the neck or back of the shoulders. The arms should not bind, and the shoulder seam should fall approximately ½ to 1 inch off the top of the shoulder. Men with very sloped shoulders, typical of heavily muscled bodies, will often have difficulty finding a ready-made shirt that fits properly. Custom-made shirts are the solution to such fit problems.

44

Symmetry

*T*HE HUMAN BODY is visually symmetrical. The body is basically the same on each side of a central vertical line (the median), creating a formal balance. A symmetrical design is the most logical and easily accepted arrangement for the elements of a garment and is therefore the most common design for apparel.

The eye corrects minor discrepancies in size and shape, so when an object is close to being symmetrical, the eye sees it as equal on both sides. Look at the jacket in the drawing on this page. Is it a symmetrical design? Actually, the jacket is asymmetrical. Your eye probably ignored the asymmetrical details. The eye follows the buttons up the center front and does not notice that the leading edge (the edge of the buttonhole side of the jacket) actually extends beyond the centerline. Since the design lines, collar, and large pockets emphasize formal balance, the effect of the design is symmetrical. Menswear is often asymmetrical, because of the preference for a single breast pocket. We are used to seeing the detail on the left. Emphasizing the asymmetry by tucking a bright pocket square or white handkerchief in the pocket give the jacket a jaunty look.

Women's garments are often designed with radically asymmetrical details. These can be structural, such as a pocket or design detail, or decorative, like a painted motif or spot trim. Truly creative asymmetrical garments must be carefully designed so the elements balance and compliment one another. Balance and proportion are more experimental in asymmetrical garments because there are fewer formulas for the placement of style lines.

Asymmetrical hemlines can create an alluring and unusual effect. The hemline should be designed to blend with the total effect of the garment and be definite enough to look like it was done on purpose, not by mistake. A diagonal hemline slims the leg but also draws attention to it. Unless your legs are attractive, avoid a tricky hem detail.

Details focus the attention of the viewer on one side of a garment. Often a large, untrimmed space on one side balances an asymmetrical detail, as in the center garment on the facing page. Asymmetrical garments are effective in camouflaging apparel for

handicapped persons, who often do not have symmetrical figures.

Symmetrical garments may be accessorized to look asymmetrical. The garment on the right shows how an asymmetrically tied scarf and off-center details add interest to a basic outfit. The scarf functions like a hairstyle parted to one side. By accenting one side, a diagonal line is created that lengthens and slims the figure. Accessories such as a bright pocket square, a boutonniere, or handkerchief worn on a blazer create a slightly asymmetrical effect and add a surprise accent to a garment that gives it wit and style.

45

Scale

*A*N EFFECTIVE GARMENT must be in harmony and balance with the figure that wears it. The garment should not overwhelm or detract from its wearer. This is particularly important for the shorter person.

Commercial missy apparel (a size range supposedly designed for the typical American woman over 20) is fitted to a model who is 5 feet 6 or 7 inches tall. This means an average classical jacket length is 26 or 27 inches at the center back. A woman under 5 feet 4 inches will be overwhelmed by this garment, because too long a garment will make her seem shorter. Specialty sizing for women who cannot wear a missy size is growing. Petite sizes are scaled down for the smaller woman. Large-size apparel is proportioned for women who wear sizes larger than a 16. In the last 5 years, these specialty categories have been made available through a growing number of retailers because demographic studies have proved that the "typical" missy customer is a smaller segment of the total population than was previously thought.

Accessories and details must be scaled down for the petite woman and emphasized for the larger figure. Large-size clothing has to be recut to accommodate the figure variation typical of sizes over 16. Professional application of design rules to make a small woman seem taller and a large woman seem trim make this apparel more appealing to the specialty customer. When a short woman is overweight, she may have to wear regular-size clothes to accommodate her girth, and have the apparel altered to flatter her height.

The most effective way to dress the short, large woman is to select garments that emphasize the vertical line of the figure and that are simply tailored with a minimum of details. Subtle textures and patterns do not define the size and space of the figure and are more flattering than spotty prints. Subtle tweed suits or small, neat patterns contrasted with soft, lustrous fabrics for blouses and accessories are good choices. Bright, heavy accessories, including wide belts, shorten the figure.

Shoes are important to continue the illusion created by the right clothes. Do not wear heavy shoes if you are petite, because they will seem out of balance with slender short legs. Trim, comfortable shoes that

Right   *Wrong*

allow one to walk naturally always give the most flattering look for any size woman. Shoes that are a tone of the skirt or a neutral color the same shade as the stockings (nude, taupe, or grey, for example) extend the leg line and make the wearer's legs seem slimmer and longer.

The woman's garments on the facing page illustrate problems of scale. You can see how the large bow, long jacket, heavy pocket detail, and bulky shoes overwhelm the petite woman. The solution is to emphasize the vertical and substitute a scaled-down jacket with smaller details and simple shoes to make the petite woman seem taller and slim. The second complicated wrong outfit causes the viewer to compare all the small details with the figure's volume and creates a confusing design that makes the figure seem larger than necessary.

Scale is less of a problem with menswear because of the slower evolution of fashion and the relatively traditional formulas that regulate styling.

Cumbersome

Well-proportioned

Overpowering

Subtle

Appropriate scale and fit are easier to achieve because menswear is sized with a greater variety of options to accommodate short men and large and tall men. In addition, alterations are expected to make menswear fit and, in fact, often are done free of charge. Pants are left unhemmed, so length is easily adjusted and can be readily altered at the waist and crotch because of the way they are constructed. Final-ly, custom tailoring has a traditional place in menswear that allows apparel to be scaled to the customer. Nevertheless, high-fashion garments that are too flamboyant or exaggerated will overwhelm the slight figure. Very large men look awkward with details that are too small or delicate and suits that are too snug.

46

Unity

NITY MEANS THAT all the elements of a design work together to produce a successful visual effect. An outfit that has been designed by one person tends to have a unified look, because a trained designer builds an outfit around one design concept. A garment that has too many points of interest, or has too great a variety of lines, or lacks a dominant theme is usually unsuccessful, because all the details compete for attention.

Men's suits frequently have a unified theme. Blending it with the tie and shirt pattern and colors as suggested in Chapter 4 can build an outfit with a unified look. Problems occur with casual apparel when each component competes as a dominant element of the outfit. The best solution is to select a basic garment to combine with a fashion piece in each outfit and not to create two competing centers of interest.

A woman often combines garments from several designers and should understand the elements of unity to create an effective outfit.

Here are some guides to help you build successful outfits.

1. *Style lines should be consistent* throughout a garment or coordinates combined within an outfit. A typical mistake is illustrated at the bottom of the page. Combining a jacket that has an off-center leading edge with a skirt that has a center detail creates an awkward jog in the lines of the complete outfit. One solution is to wear a single-breasted jacket with the front-opening skirt, or to wear the double-breasted jacket over a simple skirt without a center front seam or one with an asymmetrical opening that aligns with the leading edge of the jacket.

2. *All the areas of a garment should reflect the same shapes.* In the incorrect example at the top of the next page, the collar, cuffs, and hem are curved. The square pockets interrupt the unity of the design theme. Notice how the correct classic solution uses curved details to carry out the established theme of the garment.

3. *Curved lines are very compatible with the shape of the body.* Geometric lines and shapes are less compatible with body curves, but they can be effective and dramatic if carefully designed. An example is given of a dramatic use of geometric shapes

Wrong   *Solution*   *Same jacket*

Plain shirt

in a garment. Notice how the angle of the line at the neckline is repeated at the bottom and how the vertical is continued from the neckline to the overlap. Attention to such details creates unity in a design that involves several shapes.

4. *A small jog in a line interrupts its flow and is distracting.* For example, a small difference between the length of a sleeve and the bottom of a jacket interferes with the horizontal movement of the eye. This does not mean that all sleeves must be the same length as the jacket, but the difference should be significant enough to be a design element in itself. The wrong example is corrected by the classic solution of aligning the sleeves with the jacket hem. In the more unusual example, the contrast between the length of the sleeves and that of the jacket makes the jacket seem even shorter; that is, it serves as a design element that emphasizes the dominant theme of the outfit.

5. *Style trim should be consistent.* A decorative button is meant to be noticed. Combining a jacket that has bright gold buttons with a skirt that has contrasting plastic buttons will create a confusing outfit with two style trims clamoring for attention. Small, functional shirt buttons blend with the fabric and may be combined with many other kinds of buttons.

... Dramatic shapes and angles give interest and length

NO

Rounded pockets follow cut of the blouse, give longer look

NO

Sleeves and jacket of same length elongate the figure

47

Fabric Unity

*T*HE UNITY OF A GARMENT depends on the way fabric is used as well as on style lines. Here are a few pointers on how to select the most attractive patterns.

   1. *Stripes and plaids* that run in the same direction and are used on the straight grain should match, particularly on sleeves that hang parallel to the body. Stripes and plaids cut on the bias may be used with patterns cut on the straight grain, but the direction of all the bias pieces must match. Bold stripes are most obvious when they do not match. Stripes or plaids that run in different directions can be used to create an effective garment and to avoid the problem of matching the pattern exactly.
   2. If *a pattern and a solid fabric are combined,* the colors must be compatible. It is difficult to find an exact match between the ground color of a pattern and the solid. It is safer to combine a solid with an accent color used in the pattern, because an accent color usually does not appear as a large solid area, so an exact match is less important. However, the accent color must have enough weight in the print to make the relation to the solid color obvious.
   When matching colors, look at the whole garment. The full impact of a print or color cannot be seen on a small swatch. Compare colors in daylight. Store lighting distorts them. Do not just hold the fabrics together for a "close-up" look. You must look at the total effect of the match from a distance, because that is how it will be seen on your body. Hang the garments up, or have another person hold them, about 10 feet away. Is the blend effective from a distance? Is the accent color in a print important enough to relate to a solid companion fabric. Is the ground color of the print compatible with a solid?
   3. If *two or more patterns or textures* are used in an outfit, they should be compatible in color and design. Colors can compliment or contrast, but they must be related to one another. Patterns may be similar motifs in different colors or different motifs in the same color, but again the relation between the two should be pleasant. Positive and negative prints use the same color and pattern, with the ground color in the nega-

tive print reversing to positive. These print combinations usually are very effective.

   Train your eye to analyze how a designer unifies elements to create a successful garment. When you see an awkward-looking garment or outfit, check to see which elements are in conflict with the design theme. Perhaps there is no unifying use of fabric. This practice will make it easier for you to assemble parts of an outfit into an effective whole.

48

Rhythm

*R*HYTHM IS THE REPEATED use of line or shapes to create a pattern. Orderly repeats of a line or motif direct the eye through a design with a flowing movement.

Uniform rhythm is the repetition of the same design element. This simple formula tends to become boring if there is no variation or accent added to the design. Color can make uniform rhythm more exciting by emphasizing similar shapes or certain parts of the garment. The garment on the left of the facing page illustrates uniform rhythm. A similar shape is repeated many times in the caftan. Study the illustration before you color it as suggested. The repetition of the wedge shape is pleasant, but the total effect is not exciting. With the addition of contrasting colors, the shapes take on new meaning. They seem to radiate from a central axis that directs the viewer's attention to the face. Color provides the drama the repeated shapes lack.

Progressive or graduated rhythm is the repetition of a shape in units of increasing size. This type of rhythm builds the interest of the viewer and draws the eye through the graduated units, from the largest to the smallest. In the center garment, the eye is drawn upward as the ruffles decrease from wide to narrow. This design does not have to depend on color for its effectiveness, but a dramatic color scheme will emphasize the size of the shapes and move the eye quickly through the interesting design created by the color gradations.

Unequal rhythm is the use of unexpected spaces in a garment. It can have a dramatic effect when carefully used. The garment on the right shows a dramatic example of unequal rhythm in an evening gown. The color band would not emphasize a large bust or stomach because of the loose fit of the garment.

Men's casual wear often uses unequal rhythm to break up the space of shirt designs. Horizontal design elements at the mid-torso and shoulder emphasize the wedge silhouette, the most desirable masculine shape, so this is a favorite design theme for casual menswear.

Equal rhythm is the most static and unimaginative use of repeated space. The uniform use of space contributes to a chunky, awkward design. Unequal or graduated rhythms are usually the most interesting ways to break up horizontal space.

Careful experimentation is necessary to design a garment that has a pleasing rhythm, because the several spaces or design elements must be coordinated so they do not detract from the total garment. The difference of a few inches in the size of a space or detail is often sufficient to create an awkward design.

cream

Yellow

gold

gold

orange

Yellow

orange

hot pink

aqua

Purple

white

hot pink

black

black

49

Emphasis: Color Contrast

*E*MPHASIS MEANS CREATING a focal point by outlining or exaggertating a detail so it becomes the prominent design element on an outfit. The most obvious way to emphasis a design detail is a sharp color contrast, but unusual shapes, different textures, a bold detail on a relatively simple space, and very bright colors also emphasize a design.

Several emphasized areas in one outfit result in a disorganized and fragmented design with too many focal points. No emphasis results in a monotonous design. Interesting apparel must achieve a balance between order and detail. Too much organization creates a boring design. Too many focal points create a confused garment.

Emphasizing specific elements of a garment may strengthen the visual illusion it is designed to create. The suit on the left on the facing page is an excellent example of emphasis through outlining of the style lines. Contrasting braids or fabric bindings on the front edges of the jacket outline the vertical lines of the suit. The garment would not have as outstanding a vertical line if the jacket were trimmed in a matching binding. The loose but straight cut of the jacket adds to the vertical and can conceal a heavy bosom or a thick waist. All these design elements contribute to the illusion of slimness and height. This formula was invented by the French couturier Coco Chanel during the 1920s. She did many versions of the braid-trimmed suit throughout her career, and the style has become a classic that is continued today.

The models in the drawing are wearing the Chanel shoe. The black toe visually shortens the foot and makes it seem smaller. The heel height and sling back have been revised according to the prevailing fashion of the period, but the basic formula of light leather contrasting with a black patent leather toe has remained constant.

Positive contrast means accenting style lines with a dark braid or trim. Negative contrast is accenting a dark suit with a white or light trim. Both types of emphasis are effective for slimming the figure when they emphasize a vertical line in the outfit.

The outfit on the right uses contrasting collar and cuffs to focus attention on the face and hands. Think of a police officer directing traffic in a dark suit and white gloves, which makes the hands the most visible part of the body. Chanel often used contrast. The fresh white collar and cuffs have an ingenuous schoolgirl look. A small flower or crisp bow tie at the neck is another accent that directs the eye up the garment toward the face. White collars and cuffs are slimming when added to a simple, dark garment.

Remember that color emphasis works with accessories too. A light or bright shoulder bag calls attention to the part of the body it hang by. If your hips are large, avoid emphasizing them by wearing a contrasting shoulder bag. If your feet are large, blend shoe color with hose color and the color of your skirt. Reverse this formula if you have especially dainty feet and legs, so bright shoes highlight your best assets.

Cream

Navy

Cream
and
Navy

Cream

Navy

White

White

Navy

50

Emphasis: Design Motifs

A BOLD OR UNUSUAL SHAPE will emphasize the area it covers. Hand-painted designs on full, loose caftans and coats are typical of many hand-painted garments created by textile artists. These garments are often dramatic because of the bold use of colors and motifs to emphasize certain areas of the body.

Placement of design elements is critical to the esthetics of a garment. Casual menswear may utilize large motifs on the torso more easily than women's wear. A man's back and chest are acceptable areas to decorate with bold designs. Generally, apparel for everyday wear avoids emphasizing the crotch for both sexes. There are several other areas of a woman's body that should not be emphasized, unless for theatrical reasons: the bust, the stomach, and the derriere. Designers working with a large print often inadvertently place a motif on one of these areas. The wearer may feel uneasy about the garment but cannot understand why until she walks down the street and notices many stares focusing on her bust or derriere. Shop carefully, and use a three-way mirror to evaluate all aspects of a garment.

Theatrical costume designers reverse the rules of commercial apparel if they want to create sexy costumes, by focusing on the bust, the crotch, and the derriere. In the classic can-can outfit, the bust is accented with a contrasting color and outlined with braid. Many ethnic costumes emphasize the bust line with a tight vest cut under the bosom and worn with a contrasting blouse. Historically, these costumes developed when female fertility was economically desirable. Folk costumes unconsciously emphasize the most feminine elements of a woman's figure. Lingerie often emphasizes the bust with lace, because it is socially acceptable to wear intimate apparel that is feminine and sexy.

Designers that applique a motif on the stomach of a maternity dress are doing the expectant mother a disservice. Pregnant women should avoid wearing casual and business clothes that focus on their rapidly expanding stomachs. Maternity wardrobes should emphasize the vertical and use soft, flowing one-piece garments as their main components.

Avoid placing
a motif on any
of these areas

Bavarian
Folk-
Costume

51

Silhouette

AN APPAREL DESIGNER IS A SCULPTOR who uses the human body as an armature for soft fabric sculpture created to enhance the figure. The designer usually begins by sketching the front of a garment in two dimensions and then visualizes or constructs the back and the sides to compliment the three-dimensional shape. The size and shape of the garment are first perceived by its silhouette or outline. Then the eye of the viewer moves to the subdivisions created by the design elements to capture the total impression of the garment. These secondary elements—proportion, line, symmetry, scale, unity, rhythm, and emphasis—have just been discussed.

The silhouette is the dominant visual element of a garment and dictates most of its other design elements. The two main influences on silhouette are fashion and the individual body. Fashion cycles often focus on a specific silhouette, but many kinds of apparel are used concurrently, and people usually have a variety of silhouettes in their wardrobe at any one time. Fashion silhouettes change most drastically in women's wear. Menswear silhouettes tend to evolve more slowly, with less exaggeration. Menswear silhouettes are discussed in Chapter 62. Fashion silhouettes are modified by adding fabric and padding to various parts of the body to create a specific shape. The silhouette usually conforms to the shape of the body, but exaggeration is used to create a special effect or to emphasize a part of the body that is a current focus of fashion.

The silhouette that changes the least is the natural silhouette or basic body shape used for active wear and made from stretch fabrics. Swimwear, leotards, knit sports shirts, and shorts conform to the body and look best on an active, physically fit figure. The comfort and functionality of stretch active wear is desired by all figure types, and illusions can be created with color and pattern that flatter the less-than-perfect figure.

The principles of illusion we have discussed can change the image of a body in a natural silhouette. The sketches on these pages illustrate some of the design elements that can be used. Cutting the leg line in an upward V gives the illusion of a longer leg. Women can wear leotards with sleeves to camouflage a flabby upper arm. Dark stockings and a bright body suit empha-size the slimmer torso characteristic of a pear-shaped figure. Experiment with the amount of upper leg that should be covered with a dark color. A deep shade for the body suit and stocking slims and lengthens. (Black is not a must. Try a deep burgundy, forest green, teal, or navy for variety.)

In the garment on the left of the facing page, a bold diagonal stripe minimizes the size of the waist and bust. The color of the stockings should be determined by the size and shape of the legs. If your legs are slender and an asset, wear a light or bright color. Heavy legs will look slimmer if you wear dark stockings.

The center figure shows how a short wrap skirt or slim gym shorts worn over a leotard can camouflage large hips. A contrasting design element at the bust balances the width of the hip. Legs look longer if short socks are worn with tennis shoes.

On the right, a heavy bosom and a slender hip and leg line are balanced by wearing a simple, dark-colored leotard with a cap sleeve and a high neckline. Light stockings make the legs more prominent. Adding a vest or slim-fitted sweatshirt over the leotard would further camouflage this problem.

Low cut suit on hips makes legs seem shorter

Burgundy

Navy

Navy

Red

Navy

Red

Navy

Red
and
Black

Dark
Tights for
heavy legs.
Bright for
slim.
(Black
or
Red)

Soft
Pink

52

Natural Silhouette:
Women's Classic Bathing Suits

THE ONE-PIECE BATHING SUIT, or maillot, is a classic. It can be worn by figure types from matronly to youthful. The difference is in the inner construction of the suit and the cut of the outer shell. Fuller figures require a defined and supported bust, which may be provided by a preformed bra cup in a durable interlining fabric. Junior suits for slim figures may have no undersupport or only a soft lining shaped with elastic under the bust. Most bathing suits are made from stretchable fabrics, either an elastic knit or a rigid fabric that has been elasticized.

Color is important to emphasize body areas and to frame the skin. Bathing suit colors should enhance skin tone. Dark, rich colors and bright colors enhance a tan. White is an excellent contrast to a tanned skin, but it is difficult to make opaque when wet, so it must be used with care in the area of the crotch and bust in a bathing suit. Pastels make the skin look washed out and are not often selected for bathing suits.

Function is important when selecting a bathing suit. The wearer should be able to swim in it, and the materials should be able to stand up to the elements to which the suit is exposed. Manufacturers test new fabric in sunlight, salt water, and the chemicals most often found in a swimming pool. Elastic, trims, and underlinings also are tested to make sure they will last as long as the shell fabric.

Variations in the cut, color, or decorative details of a suit may subtly alter the appearance of the body. Suits for the heavier figure often are designed with a small skirt to hide the fullness of the hips and upper thighs. An added "tummy panel" will control a full stomach and add a design element, but should be the same color or pattern as the rest of the suit so it does not stand out. Slim legs can be made to look longer if the leg line on the suit is cut up slightly. A straight line at the crotch will make the thighs seem wider. The "boy" leg is a very short-short that stands away from the thigh and minimizes its bulk.

The suits on this page use diagonals to slim the body visually. The one on the left slims and highlights a

Slims waist

Emphasize Bust, slims hips

small waist and minimizes the bust and hips, a good choice for the hourglass figure. The other suit slims the waist and hips and emphasizes the bust, perfect for the pear-shaped figure.

In the examples on the facing page, notice how bright patterns and decorative details emphasize the bust. The blouson top camouflages a bulky waist. A skirt minimizes a protruding stomach, boxy hips, or heavy thighs. A person with a heavy bust can wear a skirt or boy-leg bottom to balance the smaller hip. Verticals narrow and slim the figure from the bust to the hips.

53

Natural Silhouette:
Women's Novelty Bathing Suits

NOVELTY BATHING SUITS depart from the classic maillot to become a great variety of innovative styles. Generally, the less suit, the more perfect the figure must be to wear it effectively. The tricks of emphasis work with two-piece suits as well as with one-piece suits, but the exposed body becomes a more dominant part of the design as it becomes more visible.

The first suit at the bottom of the page would camouflage a thick waist and make the person seem shorter because of the contrasting colors. The diagonal lines of the suit on the right slim the waist and make the bust seem fuller. The deep V makes the model seem taller.

The top bikini on the opposite page would be best worn by a very slim and well-proportioned figure. A dark binding edging the bright fabric would make the bust seem larger. The strong horizontal of the bottom makes the hips seem wider, but the vertical of the exposed body makes the legs seem longer.

The modest two-piece suit beside it would highlight a slim waist. A dark or bright solid or print fabric would emphasize the bust and hip line. The boy leg makes the upper thigh seem less full, but the legs will not seem as long.

The gathered bra top on the bottom example would fit and yet somewhat camouflage a very full bust but would also look good on a modest bust. A good fit and a dark color enhance the effect. This suit calls attention to the stomach. The legs seem longer because of the graceful, high-rise leg line.

The asymmetrical suit slims the waist and emphasizes the hip. The bust would be deemphasized by the simple top. A more structured bra top is built into this suit, accommodating a wide range of bust sizes.

Camouflages Waist

Lengthens Figure

54

Slim-line Silhouette: Women's Pants

*T*HE SLIM-LINE SILHOUETTE hugs the body. It is the classic tailored silhouette. The slim-line pants silhouette is not attractive when worn by full-figured women, because the garments fit so snugly they accent every curve of the body. Soft-dressing silhouettes are more effective for the larger woman. Pants must fit well to enhance the figure. There are two main types of tailored pants, the snug jean and the looser straight-leg trouser.

Jeans are a practical garment because of their durability and comfort. They are now available in almost every size and are even modified for maternity wear. Jeans are attractive for many figure types, but careful attention to fit is important for all women and especially those with heavy thighs or derrieres.

Jeans usually come in sturdy, heavyweight cotton twill fabric, such as 11½– to 14–ounce denim. They should fit snugly. The heavy fabric, reinforced seams, and sturdy zipper are designed to have direct contact with the figure from the thighs up. Denim tends to shrink when washed and then relax slightly when worn so it conforms to the figure. Jeans are too tight if they are uncomfortable at the crotch area, wrinkle through the thighs, gape at the zipper, or are uncomfortable to sit in. Jeans that force flesh up above the waistband are too tight.

There are no size standards for apparel, and manufacturers have a wide range of fit standards and sizing specifications. If a jean does not fit appropriately, try jeans from other manufacturers until you discover the cut that is best for you, then stick to that brand.

Many confirmed jeans wearers wash their good jeans to shrink them and then have them pressed or dry-cleaned again so they become crisp and have a defined front crease. A smoothly fitted pair of jeans will make a person look taller because of the dark color, slim fit, and vertical front creases. Worn with boots or medium-heeled shoes, jeans will make the legs seem longer and slimmer.

The legging or stretch pant is made of stretch knit fabric and often has a stirrup to hold it down. It is really

a heavy stocking, and is usually worn with a full top or under other apparel, like stockings. This pant conforms to the figure and reveals all the leg curves and is most appropriate for youthful casual garments.

The trouser often is styled with darts or release pleats to compensate for the drop (the difference in measurement between the waist and the hips). Usually, a balanced figure has a 10–inch drop. Trousers should fit smoothly over the top of the hips and fall in a straight sweep of fabric from the fullest part of the upper hip to the hem. Wools, lightweight cotton blends, and many other types of fabric may be used

Jeans

Leggings

Trousers

for trousers because the looser fit does not stress the fabric the way the snug fit of jeans does.

Pants that cling to the thighs or fit too snugly through the seat will emphasize the width of the hips and accentuate the fullest part of the figure. The front pleats and the pockets should not pull or gape. The crotch should not grab. The crotch line of a pair of well-fitted trousers should fall between 1 and 2 inches from the body. Look in a three-way mirror to check the fit of pants over the seat to make sure there are no tension lines or underwear shadows. Pants are too tight if any lines are visible. Many women elect to wear only

panty hose under pants so there are no underwear lines.

If your figure problem is a full stomach, avoid front-zipper pants. Substitute side- or back-zip pants to make this a subordinate area. Pleats that are pulled open by a tummy bulge accentuate the problem.

The illusion of height is easily created with pants and a slim, fitted blouse or sweater. Pants automatically make a person look taller because the body from the waist down is covered with a single expanse of fabric. A slightly flared pant leg will also increase the illusion of height.

55

Slim-line Silhouette: Skirted Outfits

$\mathcal{T}$HE SLIM-LINE SILHOUETTE in an outfit with a skirt is flattering for most figures because no bulk is added to the figure. The skirt must fit properly to be effective. It must not wrinkle or droop at the waistline. Designers often add elastic to the waistband to accommodate the natural expansion when a person sits down. The skirt should fit the hips and stomach area smoothly, with no hint of tension. Tension lines at the hip or across the stomach create horizontals that defeat the slimming effects of the skirt's silhouette. They make a woman seem heavier, "stuffed" into her clothing. The skirt should not cling to the derriere but should fall smoothly from the fullest part of the figure to an even hemline. The skirt should hang straight at the side seams when seen from the front. A pegged skirt, with a narrow hem, makes the hips seem wider.

Vertical style lines make a person seem taller. These can be seams or pleats but should be compatible with the styling of the top worn with the skirt.

The length of the jacket worn with a skirt is crucial to the total effect of the outfit. A jacket that is too long makes the wearer seem shorter, because the length of the skirt is visually shortened. A short woman will find a jacket that ends 3 or 4 inches below the waist is more flattering than one that aligns with the waist or is too long.

The length of the jacket also depends on the color. A contrasting jacket should be carefully balanced for length, because the body clearly will be divided into two areas. A dark skirt with a light jacket lengthens the figure. The hip area is minimized, and the eye is directed upward to the bust and face. A dark jacket worn over a light bottom shortens the figure and emphasizes the skirt. The less conspicuous division of the body by a one-color suit allows more leeway for jacket length. The person seems tallest in a one-color suit. A short jacket combined with a slim but softened skirt is an excellent proportion for the petite woman.

The tailored silhouette is also appropriate for dresses. The classic shirt dress has a slim-line silhouette. This flattering style is characterized by a front placket that carries the eye the length of the dress and tends to slim and elongate the figure. The front placket also makes this an easy garment to put on and take off. A jacket worn over the shirt dress can make a conservative business outfit. The dress is more feminine than a skirt and blouse, because it is styled in a softer fabric, often with a lustrous texture. The crisp jacket gives a businesslike character to the softer dress.

Dressmaker
Suit

Verticals
increase the
illusion of
height, and
slim the
figure

Coat Dress

56

Soft Silhouette: Women's Pants

*T*HE SOFT SILHOUETTE has more ease and a fuller fit than the slim-line silhouette. Just enough fabric is added to the silhouette so the clothing does not hug the body tightly. This is an effective silhouette for the heavier figure. The added fabric conceals the heavier torso, but there is not so much fabric that the figure is visually enlarged.

Thinner fabrics usually go with this silhouette. It is particularly comfortable in warm weather because the looser fit and thinner fabric allow air to circulate near the body. This kind of styling tends to look dressier than tailored garments. Fabrics that drape, such as knits and soft crepes, typically are used for soft dressing. Lightweight, smooth fabrics like cotton sheeting are used for casual pants with a soft fit. Details typical of tailored garments, such as structured collars and pocket flaps, usually are inappropriate, because the fabric is too light.

Shirring, pleats, tucking, and other decorative means of controlling ease are the styling devices that create soft garments. They softly arrange the fabric over the fullest part of the body, avoiding the revealing precision fit and structured seams and darts that draw attention to the body. Fabric can be carefully allocated to compensate for figure problems. A short-waisted person, for example, can make the torso seem longer with a soft top that is blousoned over a wide belt so only a portion of the belt is visible. The sketches on the next page show how effective this can be. The drape of the blouse over the belt visually extends the length of the waist.

A person with full hips should wear as slim a line as possible and select pants that fit well. Gaping pleats accentuate the stomach and hip. Too much fullness will make the figure seem larger than it is. A top with an easy fit that is styled to be worn over the pants is an attractive way of camouflaging a full waist. The over-top that has shoulder pads or dolman sleeves balances the pear-shaped figure by equalizing the shoulder line and the hip. The length of the top is an important element in the success of the outfit. Generally, a woman will look the best if the top stops slightly above the flare of the hips or (when fashionable) below the fullest part of the thighs. If a top ends at the middle of the full part of the thighs it makes even a slightly bulky figure seem larger.

The shape of the pant leg is a fashion variable. The trick is deciding how much exaggeration of the prevailing fashion most flatters your figure. Pant legs may be tapered at the ankle, straight, or flared. In moderation, tapered or flared pants will flatter most figure types. When exaggerated, they create a variety of illusions that do not flatter all figure types. The very tapered (also called pegged) pant exaggerates the hip line and makes the thighs seem large. The size of

the feet will be diminished, making feet seem smaller. This silhouette should be avoided by pear-shaped figures and other types that are heavier than normal. This silhouette balances a wedge-shaped figure, and could be quite flattering to slender balanced and wedge bodies.

Flared pants add bulk to the figure, from knees to ankles. The flare that begins at the hips will seem like a full skirt and would be flattering to most pear-shaped bodies and moderate-sized balanced and wedge shapes. A very heavy woman would be more attractive in a modified style with a slight flare. Pants that fit snugly to the knees and then flare radically should be worn by tall, slender figures, because they tend to make a person seem shorter and heavier. Flared pants minimize the size of feet. A slightly flared pant worn over a high-heel shoe camouflages the foot and makes the person seem taller.

57

Soft Silhouette: Skirted Outfits

*S*OFT SILHOUETTES mean there is additional fabric used in the styling of skirts, for example, dirndls and gathered and flared skirts. This is the most flattering silhouette for the fuller figure. The skirt avoids many problems of the soft pants silhouette, because the visible part of the leg slims the silhouette. Soft dresses and skirts are most often made in lightweight fabrics, and the fullness can look like added fabric instead of flesh. Bows, ruffles, tucks, and pleats are typical styling details for this feminine way of dressing. The moderate-skirt silhouette is basically rectangular and adapts itself to concealing a full waist or hips. It is also effective in making a tall, angular woman look more feminine. Again, the trick is the addition of soft fabrics and details to cover the angular bones and joints.

On the next page, the garment on the left illustrates the classic float, or shift. This type of dress flatters the heavier, shorter woman because the lack of waist definition gives a long line that accentuates height. Pattern and color are the most important additional elements when styling a dress to flatter the short, heavy figure. Vertical stripes lengthen and slim the figure. Deep, rich, solid tones streamline a bulky torso. Dark colors with accents at the neck and wrist direct attention to the face and hands and diminish the visual importance of a heavy body.

The soft flared skirt is one of the most flattering garments for any figure type. The flared shape is slim at the hips and fuller at the hem, which slims the legs when contrasted with the volume of the skirt. A top with a soft blouson and an understated waistline will flatter many figure types.

Details within this formula can make it more effective for specific figure types. A woman with a large bust should wear blouses with a controlled amount of ease. Gathered fabrics tend to lead the eye to the source of the gathers, so concentrate the fullness at the neck or shoulders if you have a full bosom. The woman with a smaller bust can select a garment with ease closer to the bust. The hourglass figure can make the most of a flared skirt and soft blouse by dramatizing a small waistline with a bright belt. The soft areas of the blouse and flared skirt will minimize the size of the bust and the width of the hips and balance the pear-shaped figure.

The dirndl and other gathered skirts with too much ease over the stomach will balloon out and emphasize a full stomach, especially when made in a stiff fabric. Select a skirt with no ease at the center front and some gathers at either side of the center front. Too much ease at the waistline gives a square-hip look. The dirndl skirt does not have a flared hemline, and so

it looks boxy. This is an appropriate silhouette for a very slender person who wants to look larger below the waist.

The kind of fabric and the way a skirt is cut affect the amount of fullness the skirt can effectively have. A firm, woven fabric cut on the bias will flow over the figure in a graceful flared shape, because the bias

grain of most fabrics has a natural stretch and suppleness. A bias-flared skirt in a firm fabric will hold its shape and not droop or sag. This is a good selection for a problem hip line, because it will not pull out when gathered. Soft fabrics are an excellent choice to give a full figure enough fabric to soften body lines yet not create an overly exaggerated silhouette.

58

Wedge Silhouette: Women

$\mathcal{T}$HE WEDGE SILHOUETTE increases the visual width of the body at the shoulder. Width at the shoulder makes the hips seem narrower. This illusion is heightened when the skirt or pants are slim fitting to contrast with the wider shoulders. This silhouette makes a person look taller.

The wedge silhouette for women has been popular when women have been assertive in their social roles. It was extremely popular during World War II. Women worked outside the home and assumed more responsibility for the welfare of the family while men were away in the armed forces. The late 1970s and the 1980s saw a return of the shoulder wedge as a fashion silhouette. Women were again entering the job market and assuming a more masculine role in society.

Shoulder pads do more than square the shoulder line and make a person look taller. The added construction supports the garment while it is being worn. The shape of the body has less influence on the way the garment hangs on the figure, especially a slender body. Shoulder pads also support the garment while it is on the hanger. This enhances the hanger appeal of the garment and allows the consumer to picture, before trying it on, what the garment will look like on the body.

Shoulder pads also influence garment appearance negatively. A large or ill-fitting shoulder pad will drift on the shoulder and make the garment look awkward. Shoulder pads "shadow" (are visible) through a light-colored garment and fabric. Extreme shoulder extension tends to overpower the small figure. Small women should not wear too large a shoulder pad or too puffy a sleeve. The wedge does enhance height, so it is appropriate for a petite person's wardrobe. But for the silhouette to be effective, the shoulder line must be modified to suit the height and weight of the wearer.

Garments can be styled to have a wedge silhouette by adding shoulder pads or details like full sleeves or large collars. Shoulder pads are usually smaller for a soft garment than for a tailored one. Large, puffy sleeves in crisp fabric such as taffeta or silk organza duplicate the wedge silhouette. Evening wear is often designed with "leg-o'-mutton" sleeves, and they can be quite feminine when contrasted with a slender waist detail.

Bat-wing, dolman, and raglan sleeves cut with a great deal of fabric under the arm create a wedge silhouette. This line is good for a tall woman with full bosom and slender waist and hips. The full sleeves minimize the top of the body and focus on the slim hip area. A short-waisted person can carry this silhouette if it is an unbelted or overblouse style with a long torso that visually extends the waist.

The sketch on the left above shows a tailored garment with a moderate amount of shoulder emphasis. This classic look would be appropriate for business and could be adapted for more casual apparel as well.

The soft dress in the center uses design details and sleeve shape to support the widened shoulder line. The important element of this garment is the relative narrowness of the hem line. This emphasizes the wedge shape.

The sweater on the right has a dolman sleeve and a drop-torso detail that would be appropriate for a tall woman. The emphasis on the top of the garment would tend to make a person seem smaller. A short-waisted person would camouflage this problem, because the top extends beyond the waist and has vertical lines.

59

Hourglass Silhouette

THE HOURGLASS SILHOUETTE is feminine, because it emphasizes a full bust and curvaceous hips. The narrow waist contrasts with the wider areas of the body. The hourglass figure has been a dominant theme throughout fashion history because it emphasizes the classic female shape and has cultural and historic significance as the symbol of female fertility.

In the past, waist cinchers and corsets were used to pull in the waist. Sometimes these cruel efforts to make the flexible waist area seem smaller were so harsh that women fainted or suffered broken lower ribs from being corseted. This practice made women's waists consistently smaller. During the 1960s, there was a turn toward shift dresses, and a small waistline was "lost" for about a decade. Clothing manufacturers found that women's natural waistlines had increased over an inch per size when belts returned to fashion. The decade of the '70s saw a steady increase in the sizing of garments. Manufacturers cut their clothing larger to flatter women and to emulate the more expensive houses. Women expected to wear a size smaller than usual in a better garment, and gradually all maufacturers have enlarged their clothing to new typical sizes. The chain stores are particularly emphatic about setting fit standards for the hundreds of suppliers they have. These stores publish size specifications for their manufacturers and measure the garments they order to make sure they conform to their specifications. General merchandise in department stores and specialty stores will vary widely in fit.

The visual illusion of a small waistline is still possible through design techniques similar to those used in the past, but without the severe corseting. A contrasting belt defines the waistline. Color the belt black in the left-hand sketch on the next page. The waistline recedes and seems smaller. Color the center belt a bright red or hot pink. These advancing colors will catch the eye and focus attention on the smallness of the slim waist. However, the brightness would make a thick waist more noticeable, so a bright belt is a good selection only if you have a slim waist. Remember, always use neutral, subtle shades to minimize the areas you do not wish to call attention to. Highlight the positive with bright, contrasting, or advancing colors.

The hourglass effect is enhanced by a longer-than-knee-length skirt. The sweep of a long, flared skirt makes the waist seem even smaller, and, of course, the person seem taller. A fitted waistline, a slightly fuller sleeve, and a very full skirt constitute an evening and wedding gown formula that has been successful for many years because of its femininity.

Petite women may wear the hourglass silhouette, but they should modify the proportion and the volume of the skirt so they are not overwhelmed. A small wom-

an with a full bosom will find this look unflattering. She will seem very short waisted and should not attract additional attention to her waist with a snug, contrasting belt. A woman with a bulky torso or a large waist should select another silhouette.

The hourglass silhouette can be attractive as a pants outfit. Soft pants and peplum top, accented with a wide belt, will create this illusion. This silhouette should be worn by a tall, well-proportioned person.

60

Full-volume Silhouette: Skirted Outfits

*T*HE FULL- OR EXTREME-VOLUME SILHOUETTE is occasionally popular, usually as a reaction to the conservative "ladylike" fashions of a period. Radical silhouettes often originate when avant-garde, experimental designers want to make an original statement to set themselves apart from the acceptable clothing forms promoted by commercial fashion designers. Designers often create dramatic "showpieces" to establish a new ideal of beauty or a new clothing concept to shock people into trying something new, and to attract the attention of the press. These statements reflect social trends, and the garments must be modified for sale to the mass market. Radical fashions usually are inappropriate for the business world.

The figure is minimized in the full-volume silhouette, and the draping and design of the fabric become most important. A mix of prints and textures can be used as the figure becomes less visible and the decorative elements of fabric and design take over. Several layers may be worn to achieve the mix of fabric and the full look. Lighter fabrics have movement and can be styled into several layers to create the illusion of fabric bulk and not body bulk.

Large women have a variety of wardrobe choices when fashion decrees that fullness is beautiful. A simple garment with graceful, flowing lines will be most effective for a very large figure. This woman tends to wear an extreme-volume silhouette out of necessity, even when slimmer fashions are in style. Light fabrics controlled with gathers and tucks will flow over the bulges and camouflage the bulk of the upper arms or thighs. Skirts are most flattering for the very large figure. Caftans are popular because of their long continuous line that covers the body without attempting to fit any area snugly. Caftans are best worn for casual events at home. They are inappropriate for street or business wear. Color and accents can be used dramatically, but they should focus attention on the appropriate areas of the body. Scarves worn at the neck and shoulders accent a pretty face. Jewelry can provide contrast in the outfit and direct attention to the

face or hands. Tonal hose slims the legs and provides a good contrast for the width of the skirt, which should be long enough to cover the fullest part of the calf.

The full-volume silhouette is an acceptable, classic theme for outerwear, even when the slim-line silhouette is fashionable for other clothing. Bulk conveys the impression of warmth as well as physically providing it. Furs, heavy wools, down- or fiber-filled quilts,

and heavy leathers are typical cold-weather outer layers. Bulky sweater knits worn over wool shirts and long skirts are popular during the winter. Coats are voluminous enough to cover suits and dresses. Capes and large shawls are popular additional accessories.

The petite woman will have to balance the size of her clothes and accessories to achieve the look of volume without being overwhelmed by her clothing when full volume is in fashion or when selecting bulky outerwear. If you are petite, wear a slightly shorter skirt. Keep the colors of all the components of an outfit in one tone. Choose smaller handbags and scarves. To appear taller, wear boots or stockings and shoes that match the color of your skirt. Select a medium-bulk fur with a slim style. Contrast a bulky outerwear wrap with slender skirts and tops.

61

Full-volume Silhouette: Women's Pants

*T*HE EXTREME-VOLUME SILHOUETTE is difficult for most figures to wear when fashion decrees that pants should be cut very full. This silhouette emphasizes the width of the hips and legs and makes a person seem shorter, so only a tall, slender woman can effectively wear full pants. The most successful way for others to wear the full-volume silhouette is to modify it so as to keep the volume above the hip line and contrast it with slim-line pants. Dark pants will make a person seem taller, even when she wears a bulky top. This modified silhouette is the typical cold-weather active-wear outfit. A parka or bulky sweater is worn over slim-line pants for mobility when skiing or running.

The outfit on the left is an effective combination of a full jacket and a slim pant. The eye accepts the bulk for warmth and does not read it as exaggerated. The slim line of the pants establishes the existence of a small body. The longer jacket with only the slimmer lower leg showing is good camouflage for a full torso and upper leg.

Large women sometimes wear bulky pants hoping the fabric volume will hide their figure. A better solution is to wear straight-leg pants combined with a loose tunic, vest, or jacket that covers the thighs. One deep, rich color or a neutral tone-on-tone combination is the most flattering. Bright accents added at the face and hands are attractive. The additional layer visually lengthens the torso and avoids focusing attention on the midriff. The continuous line of the pants will make the large person seem taller, yet the derriere will be covered, usually a problem area for the larger woman. The center example shows how effective this combination is for the very large woman.

Full-volume summer clothing is often made from lightweight fabrics gathered at the waist or worn loose enough to allow air to circulate near the body to keep it cool. The outline of the body is often visible through the sheer fabric, and even though the garments are full, the illusion of the body is slender. This is a very sensual look and is appropriate for many figure types.

The diversity of silhouettes usually found in an individual's wardrobe reflects both the many activities in

which the person participates and the changes in the fashionable silhouette. Most people do not regularly purchase an entirely new wardrobe, but use older components worn with newer garments to create fashionable and functional outfits. People with figure problems often dress in silhouettes based on a formula that is successful for them and modify it slightly to conform to current fashion dictates.

62

Menswear Silhouettes

*A*PHYSICALLY FIT MAN has well-developed shoulders and upper torso and a slender waistline approxiximately 10 inches smaller than the chest. This natural wedge silhouette is the traditional menswear silhouette. Suit and sports coat details subtly emphasize the wedge silhouette. For men who lack a natural wedge-shaped body, tailored business clothes are carefully constructed to create this silhouette: Shoulders are padded and inner construction forms tailored jackets whose inherent structure camouflages figure variations.

As mentioned, the sack suit (also called the American cut) is most appropriate for a stocky figure, the Continental cut can be worn by a tall, slim man, and the English, or Saville Row, silhouette has a natural but firm shoulder line and a comfortably fitted waist that can be modified for many figure types. Extreme fashion may modify the tailored silhouette into an exaggerated wedge shape. This suit requires more shoulder padding, a wider lapel, and pleated trousers and is difficult for short, stocky men to wear effectively. High-fashion silhouettes usually are ineffective for serious business wear.

The natural silhouette typically is worn for casual menswear. Knit garments are not padded, have no inner construction, and follow the contours of the natural body. Visually, they may emphasize the masculine figure type by having ornamentation (stripes, design motifs, extended shoulder lines or details) on the upper torso that creates a wedge silhouette. A woven sports shirt is less figure revealing than a knit, and will visually smooth figure bulges or camouflage the very thin or very full figure. Casual pants should fit without tension lines. Pleated styles are most effective on slim, average-to-tall men. Simple details with a moderate pegged or straight leg is the most versatile for a variety of figure shapes. Color-coordinated tops and bottoms make a person look taller. To increase height, select a shirt several tones lighter than the pants. Bright tops, patterns, and contrast colors are effective for the average-to-tall man.

Men's athletic wear usually has a natural silhouette. Swim trunks should be selected for figure types using many of the rules applied to women's wear. A boxer-style short will be most appropriate for a full fig-

Natural Silhouette

Soft Silhouette

Full Volume

ure. Boxer shorts with a short leg length make a man's legs seem longer. A bikini, because it is so revealing, is worn most effectively by a slim, physically fit person.

The full-volume silhouette is accepted for outerwear for cold-weather, casual and active sportswear. Layering the torso is the most effective way to dress for cold climates. The layer closest to the body should be a natural fiber that is absorbant (cotton and silk are the best). A knit fabric is the most comfortable because it has total mobility. The second layer should be a woven

garment that holds the warm air trapped by the knit layer close to the body and cuts the penetration of wind and cold. The final layers can be woven or knit. Bulky garments, reinforced with down or fiber fill, or leather and fur are the warmest. Warm jackets and sweaters are bulky, and when worn with slim pants they reinforce the masculine wedge silhouette. They also tend to make a person seem shorter. Avoiding contrasting colors and too much bulk will make a man seem taller.

63

Fabric

THE WAY A COMMERCIAL DESIGNER selects fabrics is the way you should select your wardrobe, using as criteria price, esthetics, season, fashion influences, and suitability for a specific purpose. Designers are trained to see a piece of fabric and imagine how it will look when sewn into the kind of garment they are designing. The successful home sewer must develop this talent also.

When purchasing ready-to-wear, the consumer has the advantage of being able to see how the fabric works for a particular garment. Even so, you should still consider the following things about the fabric before deciding to purchase a garment:

1. *Fiber.* Is the fabric suited to the season? Will it perform well and be easy to take care of? Are you allergic to it?
2. *Weight.* Is the garment the correct weight for your wearing requirements? Will it be appropriate for the season and climate? Is it too specialized for typical weather? That is, will it be wearable only for a very short season?
3. *Texture, or hand.* Is the fabric the correct stiffness for the garment? Does it drape well? Does it have a pleasant feel (called fabric *hand*)?
4. *Surface interest.* Does the color, pattern, and texture of the fabric please you? Does the fabric flatter you? Does it combine with the other colors in your wardrobe?

Winter Weight

Summer Weight

Wool—darker colors

Cotton-Linen Blend

These four elements determine the character of the fabric. They also dictate many of the limits on styling. The designer who created your garment is familiar with all types of fabric. You, as a consumer, can evaluate a garment's potential use and life according to how the fabric has performed for you in the past.

Designers try to select fabrics with current fashion appeal. Usually, a new fabric trend begins in designer clothes and expensive ready-to-wear. Like the style, the fabric is adapted for the mass market and imitated in other fibers and constructions when possible. Lightweight fabrics are in fashion for soft clothing and when silhouettes are voluminous. Tailored, smooth fabrics are popular for more structured apparel,

where construction details are important. Textured suitings and tweeds are in vogue when women's wear is fascinated with menswear.

Menswear is guided by tradition, including what types and patterns of fabrics are appropriate for various end uses. Suiting fabrics are identified as heavyweight (for cold weather), medium weight (for cool but temperate climates), and summer or tropical weight. Shirtings have traditional end uses. End-on-end cottons, fine lawns, and pima cottons are more formal shirt fabrics, while oxford cloth is suitable for more casual business applications and leisure wear. Knits are typically used for sportswear. Smooth, high-

Suedes and leathers are popular for Fall casual clothing

Dressy fabrics are often light-weight and lustrous

twist fabrics like poplin and gabardine are very versatile and appropriate for trans-seasonal wear.

Specific fabrics are typical for apparel categories. Lustrous, metallic fabrics are used for women's dressy apparel. Stretch knits are popular for active wear. Wools are typical for suits and expensive sports-wear. Cottons are appropriate for many categories of apparel, from men's shirtings to children's wear.

Color is the first thing that attracts a shopper. The next instinct is to reach out and touch the fabric. Esthetics combined with practicality are the most important aspects of selecting the right fabric for your wardrobe.

64

Fibers

*F*IBERS ARE SPUN INTO YARNS that are woven or knitted to produce fabrics. The natural fibers are cotton, wool, silk, linen, and hair fibers such as cashmere and camel's hair. Traditionally, these fibers have been considered appropriate for a specific season. Wool and the hair fibers are made into fall and cold-weather fabrics. The natural crimp in these fibers makes them easily woven or knitted into lofty fabrics that trap a layer of warm air close to the skin to protect the body against cold. Smooth, lightweight versions of wool-fiber fabrics are gabardine and challis, which can be worn in all but the hottest climates.

Silk can be worn year-round, though often as a blouse under a warmer garment in the fall and winter. It is also the most versatile dressy fiber for women's special occasion apparel.

Linen and cotton are warm-weather fibers, because they are cool, absorbent, and easily washed. Cotton can be woven into a heavy fabric, such as bulky corduroy, that can be worn for cooler temperatures.

Synthetic fibers have been developed to imitate natural fibers. Rayon, polyester, and nylon are typical. These are then woven to resemble natural fabrics.

Synthetics may be blended with natural fibers to increase the resemblance to the feel and characteristics of a natural fabric.

The choice of fiber is important when you consider how you will take care of a fabric. Wash-and-wear or easy-care characteristics are generally built into polyester fabrics. Easy care is particular important for garments that will be laundered frequently, like children's wear and work clothes and uniforms. Rayon, even though it is a cellulose fiber like cotton and linen, usually is not as durable as the natural fibers and will not stand up to constant washing.

Some fibers react badly to water and must be dry-cleaned. Wool and silk usually are dry-cleaned, although some fabrications of these fibers may be hand washed and ironed if care is taken to use a mild detergent and the proper washing and ironing temperatures. Wool tends to shrink, and therefore usually is dry-cleaned. Some silks are very fragile and will spot or discolor if they are washed improperly. Fabrics that have been colored with *fugitive* dyestuffs (meaning they will bleed and discolor other fabrics) must be dry-cleaned. Carefully read the care label sewn into each

Bulky Knit

Medium Weight

Light Weight

Cool Weather

Medium Weight - Year-round

Warm Weather

Silk: Suitings: light & medium weight

Wool: Lightweight gabardine, challis, knit jersey

Cotton & Blends: Poplin, corduroy, velveteen, shirting, twills, denim

Wool: Flannel, heavy gabardine, fleece, knits, melton tweeds

Silk: Lustrous foulards, dark prints

Cotton: Flannel, velvet, synthetic blends to resemble above.

Cotton & Cotton Blends: gauze, eyelet, T-shirt knits, seersucker, georgette, gingham

Linen: handkerchief & suiting

Synthetic: Lightweight polyester, poly-rayon blends, blends to resemble above.

garment before you make any purchase, and decide if the use of the garment will be compatible with the care you have to give it.

Leather is increasingly popular as a clothing material. Leather is expensive to begin with, and maintaining it adds even more to the cost. Because it may fade when cleaned, it is often redyed as a part of the cleaning process. Leather pants and skirts stretch and often have to be altered after frequent wear. Leather combined with fabric may limit the way such a garment may be cleaned. Consider these maintenance costs carefully when purchasing a leather garment.

Structured garments ordinarily must be dry-cleaned, because many different fabrics are used in their construction. The outer (or shell) fabric, lining, interfacings, and padding all may have slightly different care requirements. Dry cleaning is the only process suitable for all of them.

Knits can be made from any fiber and in a variety of weights, textures, and patterns. A well-constructed knit has stretch and recovery so that it does not lose its original shape. The yarns should have sufficient "twist" so they do not rub and pill. Most wool sweater yarns have a good natural twist, but some of the hair yarns like mohair, are easily damaged and subject to pilling (small balls of fiber attach to the surface of the fabric). Nylon and acrylic yarns, especially those that have been brushed, pill easily.

65

Weight and Hand

THE WEIGHT OF A FABRIC is an important consideration, especially when a durable garment is being purchased. Heavier fabrics suitable for women's pants, skirts, and jackets are called bottom-weights. Heavyweight men's suitings are called winter-weight fabrications. Blouse weights are lighter fabrics best used for women's wear blouses and dresses. Men's shirtings or shirt-weight fabrications correspond to blouse weights. Medium-weight men's suitings are suitable for cool weather, and tropicals are lightweight enough to be worn in hot weather. The fabric weight should suit the garment style and the season for which it is intended. To get the most out of your wardrobe, select as many medium-weight fabrics as possible, and use them in layers to adapt them to temperature changes.

Tailored garments, such as jackets and coats, must be made in a fabric heavy enough to support the tailored details. If the fabric is too thin, seams will show through when they are pressed, pockets will show as ridges in the shell fabric, and bound buttonholes will be lumpy.

Light, transparent fabrics used in women's wear often require a lining or a full slip, which makes the garment more expensive. Lightweight fabrics can be bonded to give them greater bulk and substance. A thin layer of fabric or foam is *laminated* (glued under pressure and heat) to the wrong side. The fabric and the bonding material may separate during cleaning and washing if the bonding process is poorly done or the wrong adhesive is used. Bonded fabrics simulate more expensive fabrics, and typically are used in the moderate-to-budget markets.

Hand refers to the feel of the fabric. Hand can be greatly altered by the kind of finish applied to the fabric. A crisp finish may give a fabric enough body so it can be used as a bottom-weight. The same fabric with a dress finish will be soft and will drape more fluidly. Finishes break down when pressed, cleaned, or worn. Generally, less expensive fabrics are finished to create a crisper hand and more body. A well-constructed fabric will have natural body that will not require excessive finishing.

A fabric's hand greatly influences the way it can be styled. A primary rule of design is to style garments in a fabric that is compatible with the silhouette desired. A fabric that is fluid and soft cannot be used for a crisp, well-tailored blazer unless it has a great deal of interlining and inner construction. The silhouette of a garment reflects the body shape if a fabric with a soft hand is used. A fabric that drapes well will fall gracefully and cling to the body. More gathering can be used with a soft fabric, and the garment will not become bulky, puffy, or awkward. A crisp fabric, like linen or sailcloth, can be used for a well-defined, tailored silhouette. A stiff interfacing would be used to add more structure to areas such as the collar, cuffs, and plackets. Interfacing may be used in draped garments, but a very light weight is appropriate to be compatible with the hand of the soft fabric.

Here are some adjectives used to describe fabric hand and texture:

- ▼ *Dry:* grainy, resilient texture typical of linen.
- ▼ *Slick; wet:* slippery texture, typical of acetate surah.
- ▼ *Crisp:* characteristic of a sized (starched) fabric such as organdy or silk organza.
- ▼ *Boardy:* stiff fabric; a derogatory term for a cheap fabric with too much sizing.
- ▼ *Gutsy:* fabric with a great deal of body.
- ▼ *Lofty:* fabric with a high pile or nap, such as velvet.
- ▼ *Flat:* weave with low surface interest, such as poplin.
- ▼ *Rough:* heavily textured surface, such as a raw silk.
- ▼ *Crepey:* light-textured surface, typical of crepe de chine.

Soft

Pearl grey

Tailored

Silver

Pearl grey

Mangold

66

Pattern: Scale

*T*ASTE IN PATTERNS to adorn the body is as individual as fingerprints, and there is no absolute right or wrong to their selection. Taste develops as you grow. A favorite childhood garment may inspire a fondness for a special kind of pattern. Ethnic and geographical origins influence pattern preference. Exposure to art trends, interior design, and other visual stimuli modifies taste. Taste is a result of unconsciously analyzing all the sensory input accumulated during a time period and applying it to specific choices of colors or patterns in apparel and home furnishings.

Scale means the size of the pattern. A pattern should be compatible in scale with the garment it is made into and with the size of the wearer. A large, dramatic print would be effective on a simple architectural garment or one that has a great deal of fabric.

A large print on stiff fabric seems bolder than one on soft fabric. For example, chiffon prints often are very large; but because of the transparency and fluidity of the fabric, the impact of the print is softened. A dramatic print that is large or colored in bold contrasts can be beautiful if the garment is designed to show off the print effectively, and if the wearer wants to stand out—and can carry it.

A petite woman will be overpowered by a large, boldly colored print, but a taller person could wear it effectively. A large print that is softly colored in neutrals or harmoniously blended shades is most versatile. It does not have the power of bold coloring yet still can have a great deal of impact. It would be a good choice for a shorter person who want to dress dramatically.

Small-scale prints are more versatile. They can be worn by petite as well as large women. A closely spaced print will seem more like a tone of color than a collection of individual motifs. Prints that consist of small, definite, widely spaced motifs look out of scale on a large woman. The eye tends to register unconsciously the number of designs it takes to cover the body, so the bulk of the person's body is emphasized by the small unit of the print.

Patterns that have the effect of textures rather than distinct print units are effective on many figure types. These include moire patterns, tweeds, subtle plaids, houndstooth, small ginghams, small dots, and

This bold, high contrast pattern would be best on a larger woman.

This softly colored print on chiffon could be worn by petite, as well as average or tall women.

Small, spaced patterns make a heavy person seem larger. A soft all-over print is more flattering to a large figure because it does not as specifically define the space.

Purple

Hot Pink

Purple

Hot Pink

Subtle combination of Purple and Magenta

fine stripes. These motifs are "no-pattern patterns" and, like closely spaced prints, they create the illusion of soft color.

Evaluate how a print looks by shopping carefully. Try on the garment in a large, well-lit dressing room, and stand back from the mirror to evaluate the overall effect of the garment. Wear makeup that is strong enough to balance the effect of bold colors, if that is your choice. Step 3 feet away from the mirror, and check to see whether the print is so large and bold that it detracts from your face. Then evaluate the effect of the garment 10 feet from the mirror and then at 20 feet or more. Beware of spots of color that emphasize unflattering parts of the anatomy. The garment that successfully passes this careful test will be a good investment.

67

Pattern Motifs

*P*ATTERN MOTIFS CAN ORIGINATE from many sources. Nature is one of the primary sources for print inspiration. Flowers, leaves, animals and other natural objects are stylized, simplified, and combined in an infinite variety. The imagination of the artist can provide a wealth of ways to arrange geometric shapes into prints and patterns such as stripes, plaids, and checks. Many geometric patterns are derived from the rich tradition of woven textiles, that is, created by the constraints of a loom and the typical crossing of yarns in a square or twill pattern.

Traditional men's suit patterns are pinstripes (very narrow vertical lines evenly spaced a short distance apart), chalk stripes (heavier vertical lines, lighter in color than the ground, with a wider spacing than pinstripes), and Prince of Wales checks (a subtle, monotone plaid). Sports coats were a sign of wealth during the nineteenth century, because they identified the urban businessman wealthy enough to have a country estate. Early sports coats had back and shoulder vents to allow more freedom when riding and shooting a hunting rifle. Bold tweeds and plaids in medium- to heavyweight wool were used for early sports jackets, and the tradition continues today. Classic patterns are the shepherd's check, Harris tweed, Donegal tweed, herringbone, and houndstooth. Men's classic tie patterns fall into three distinct groups: stripes (developed from English school colors), sports motifs (including foulards, crests, and symbols), and paisleys. The general term to describe this variety of patterns is *haberdashery.*

The menswear classics often are reinterpreted and recolored for women's wear and form a basic repertoire of patterns that are classics.

Embroidered surfaces are more typical of fabrications used for women's wear. These include appliqués, embroidery stitching, and the interweave of thread for a fabric that looks like lace. The patterns created by any of these techniques range from freeform and fanciful to disciplined and geometric. Monotone embroidery is subtle and delicate with a feminine look. Colorful, ethnic embroidery works like a printed pattern.

Engineered prints—for example, border prints—are designed to fall on a specific part of the garment.

Women's wear designers use this motif to highlight part of the garment and part of the body. A border placed at the hemline makes a woman seem shorter, because the eye of the viewer is drawn toward the bottom of the skirt. A border placed at the neckline focuses attention on the face. A border that runs up the front of a shirt emphasizes the bust and leads the eye to the face. Careful attention should be paid to the way these prints are cut, because they can call attention to a problem portion of the anatomy rather than having a flattering effect.

A print or pattern in a design that faces in one direction is called a *one-way pattern*. It should be cut so it can be viewed logically on the body. A one-way pattern cut "upside-down" looks peculiar. Most print designers alternate design units in opposite directions. The *two-way pattern* can be cut in either direction.

Shepherd's Check

Houndstooth

Prince of Wales Check

Pinstripe

Chalkstripe

Fanciful Collage of Traditional Menswear Patterns

Stripes used in various directions on a single garment can create an effective pattern. When a garment has vertical stripes it can make a person seem taller and slimmer. Bias or horizontal stripes used in contrast to the vertical stripes can form a border or contrasting design.

Bayadere prints have a "loose" stripe effect that runs across the fabric. This effect must be planned carefully, because it is often so subtle that the stripes are visible only from a distance. The hazy stripe effect could unintentionally enlarge or focus attention on the wrong area of the body.

68

Patterned Fabrics

THERE ARE SEVERAL EXCELLENT REASONS to wear patterned fabrics. First, patterns can camouflage a figure problem by providing textural and pattern interest that detracts from the size and shape of the body. Second, the pattern and the colors can help coordinate solid-colored pieces of an outfit and pull together unusual color combinations. A final reason, and probably the most important, is that you find it appealing and want to use it to decorate your body.

Certain prints are typically printed on certain fibers. Calico prints, for example, are usually printed on smooth cottons and are appropriate for warm-weather garments and children's wear. Calicos have a naive, country look and are printed in primary brights or soft, neutrally tinted florals. Foulards and paisleys are more versatile motifs that are printed on a variety of fabrics, from silk to wool challis to informal cotton. A subtle print can look dismal on a matte-finish fabric with no natural luster. The same print will be sophisticated and lustrous when printed on a rich silk or silk-like synthetic.

The blend of colors in a print can be used to pull two solid-colored garments together. The "weight," or overall coloration, of the print should be softer or slightly lighter than the solid colors with which it is worn. Distance is the most effective way for evaluating the compatibility of prints and solids in your wardrobe. Do the colors blend well? Is one piece of the outfit so bold that it fights the other, more subtle elements? This evaluation is usually easier to make if you are not wearing the clothes, because your personality is not a part of the evaluation. As we have said before, never match prints and solids by looking at small pieces of the fabrics. Colors may seem compatible close up but be very different from afar. Even experienced apparel designers hang their outfits in view, to study them and determine the visual compatibility of the components.

Patterns acquire a personality when made up into a specific garment. Fashion often decrees a specific type of pattern for a specific kind of apparel. For example, a small-to-medium-sized monotone in neutrals or medium brights looks matronly when cut into a garment for a large, mature figure and matched with conservative pants and jacket. The same pattern in a small, trim garment designed for the junior market will have a totally different personality.

Public appearances, in front of a large group or on television, require especially careful selection of apparel. Patterns are often difficult to wear in such situations, because they appear faded from a distance or are so bold they distract from your words and personality. Dress in several outfits and test them yourself before deciding on an outfit for a public appearance. Remember that you want to look chic, in control of the situation, and appropriately dressed for the occasion. Your outfit should only set the stage for your words and personality. Too bold an outfit will distract the attention of your audience and render your words less effective.

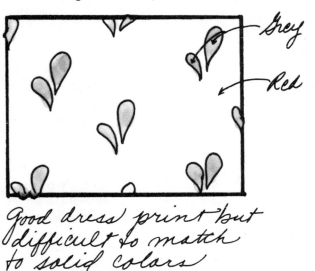

Grey
Red

Good dress print but difficult to match to solid colors

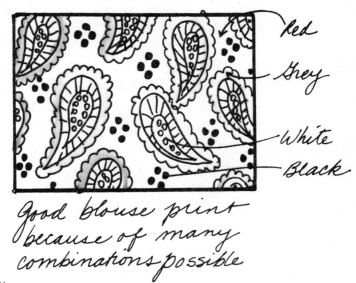

Red
Grey
White
Black

Good blouse print because of many combinations possible

Cream

Burgundy,
Cream and
Navy

Beige
ground

Navy

Burgundy

Navy

Cream

Prints and patterns breaks up the space on
a figure and can camouflage some figure
problems if the print is appropriate.

69

Pattern Combinations

COMBINING TWO PATTERNS in one outfit is more difficult to do successfully than combining plain and patterned fabrics. Patterned surfaces make a more complicated visual mix.

Here are some guidelines for the successful combination of patterns:

1. *Select patterns that are unified by color and design.* An effective combination is the use of positive and negative versions of one pattern. A positive print is one in which a colored design is printed on a white or light-colored ground. A negative print of the same pattern simply reverses the coloring—the light color is used for the design, and the original design color becomes the ground. The unit of color and motif and the elements of contrast work to create an interesting yet controlled combination.

2. *Patterns may be different but should be compatible.* There is no right or wrong, no formula. The talented designer can select a small pattern that is relief for a large, bold design. The small pattern might be used on the trim and details of the garment as a contrast to the large print. Most important is that these patterns be colored in a related scheme, either a blend of colors or a sharp contrast. Geometric patterns are a natural for combinations. Stripes and dots that share colors often are designed as "twin" prints.

3. *The fabrics on which different patterns are printed should be compatible.* The prints should be printed on a similar fabric so there are not too many diverse elements to confuse the design.

4. *The different prints should not be so similar the combination appears to have occurred by mistake* instead of by design. Make sure the prints compliment each other in color, motif, scale, and fabric.

A combination of several prints can be dramatic. In women's wear, dresses by Diane Freis all are styled in contrasting prints. Fanciful combinations of prints and trims are styled into soft, dressy print dresses quite successfully. Chic men's formal and informal business wear combines two prints and a solid well. More patterns than that gives the eye no chance to rest, and confusion is the result.

The combination of prints and fabrics with rich surface textures deserves the same careful consideration as the combination of two prints. It is particularly important to view the combinations at a distance. Multicolored textured fabrics like tweeds and textured knits take on subtle colorations that only show up at a distance.

70

Foundations: The Bra

UNDERGARMENTS ARE CALLED *FOUNDATIONS,* because they shape or contain parts of the body and affect the way clothes worn over them look. A slim, active body with a youthful, uplifted bosom needs only a few, lightweight foundations. Corrective foundations are important for heavier figures and to balance underendowed figures.

The bra is the most important foundation a woman with a large bust should wear. A bra should fit the rib cage snugly. A bra that is too tight will force flesh into an unsightly roll; a bra that is too loose will not support the bosom. The back strap should align with the base of the bosom around the body and not hike up. Tightening the shoulder straps too much will pull up the back strap rather than raising the bust, because the bust has a natural level that cannot be substantially altered. When the straps of a bra lose their elasticity, it is time to replace the bra.

Wash your bras in mild suds and air-dry them, for detergents and high heat from a dryer would shorten the life of the elastic. Perspiration also attacks the elastic in a bra and should be removed by frequent washing.

For daily wear, select bras that are close to your skin color. Colored or white bras may be attractive when worn alone, but they tend to show through clothes. Undergarments should not be seen—only their effects are important.

The proper way to put on a bra is to bend over from the waist and let your bosom fall naturally into the cups of the open bra. Then snap the bra closed and stand up. In a brassiere that is the proper size, your bust should feel contained and comfortable.

There are many different kinds and cuts of bras. The two main types are *minimizers,* which are styled to fit very large bosoms, and *maximizers,* which add fullness to a small bust. Women with a large bosom must pay the greatest attention to the fit and style of their foundations. Several specialists construct minimizers. Berle, Edith Lance, Bali, Warners, and Lily of France are some. A minimizer is cut with a wider cup that spreads the flesh to the side instead of projecting it forward. A wider shoulder strap is generally necessary to give more support, to take some of the pull from the front and back of the torso, and to ease the pressure on the shoulder. Straps may be cushioned for added comfort. A bra that closes in the back is best for a full bosom. A full figure should select a strapless bra that has a long line to the waist, because that gives more support and control. The minimizers are often boned or wired for additional support.

The woman with a small or average bosom has a greater variety of bra styles to choose from. Underwire bras are also excellent for a small bosom, because they have support under the bust and a smooth or ornamental cut but no extra bulk or wide support straps. Maximizer bras may have a fiber-filled cup to fill out the entire bust area. Small pads under the cups also enhance a bosom.

The natural look is important in foundations today. The bra cup should have a natural, rounded shape that reflects the bust shape and avoids any pointed or artificial shapes. Seamless bras provide a smooth underlayer for most clothing and are available in styles suited to most bosom sizes. Athletic bras are constructed with extra support, needed during vigorous exercises.

A kiss of death for any garment is to have a bra strap showing. Examine your outfit carefully before leaving the dressing room, to make sure your bra does not show through the outer garment and that your straps do not show. If they do, change your foundation so it remains unseen.

Strap should fit horizontally, and not hike up snap on loosest snap when new, tighten with wear

No rolls or bulges

Straps should feel comfortable and not cut shoulders

Flesh colored underwear is more practical under clothes and not as visible under sheer fabrics

Bra cup should fit smoothly, with no wrinkles or tension

Black is more glamorous unclothed and contrasts well with light skin tones

71

Other Foundations

THE UNDERPANTS YOU WEAR are most important when fitting pants. A simple brief or bikini or panty hose is sufficient for a slim figure. Panty hose worn alone gives the smoothest line under pants or a slim skirt. A bikini is comfortable, but may cause a shadow line in light-colored pants or skirts. Underpants that are trimmed with lace or contrasting appliqués may also create a shadow line under snug pants. All your underpants should fit smoothly, but not so snugly they cut into the flesh and create a bulge.

Try on a pair of fitted pants, and carefully analyze your figure from the waist down. This is the critical test to determine if you need more control in your foundation garments. Use a three-way mirror, and pay particular attention to your derriere and stomach. You should consider additional control if there are bulges of flesh that detract from the smooth line of your pants.

Control-top panty hose are the least cumbersome type of foundation to wear. They should fit smoothly and not grab at the crotch. The legs of the panty hose should be long enough so there is no stress pulling the legs up and so the crotch is still in contact with flesh. To put on panty hose for maximum comfort and to avoid damaging them, gather each leg with both hands and slip the toes of one foot into the bottom of the stocking. Gently unroll the stocking as you pull it up your leg, until you have reached the upper thigh. Repeat with the other leg. Finally, pull the waistband of the panty hose to mid-hip, and smooth the crotch area upward close to your body. Keep your fingernails and toenails smoothly filed to avoid snagging the delicate hose. You may wish to tuck your blouse in before adjusting the waistband of the panty hose at your natural waist. This will keep the blouse in place and smooth the transition of the extra layer of fabric into the bottom.

A girdle may be necessary for greater figure control. Work with a knowledgeable salesperson to select a girdle or a panty girdle. Do not just look at the way the girdle fits. Take the extra time to slip on a pair of pants or a slim skirt to determine the effect the undergarment gives the shell fabric. Select a girdle with the exact amount of figure control you need, remembering that a girdle will not decrease your overall volume but will smooth out the figure's bulges and give you a sleeker appearance.

Girdles should be hand-washed in cold water and air-dried. Use a mild soap and an elastic conditioner to extend the life of the garment. Drying in an electric dryer will rapidly destroy the elasticity of a girdle.

There is a wide range of other control garments available that may be appropriate for a special garment. An all-in-one body smoother will provide a bra and some stomach control and is especially effective under a sleek dress.

Select slips that are appropriate to the garment you are wearing. Some dresses are made in sheer,

The pant should fit without tension lines or underwear marks. In a classic trouser the fit should be trim and not baggy.

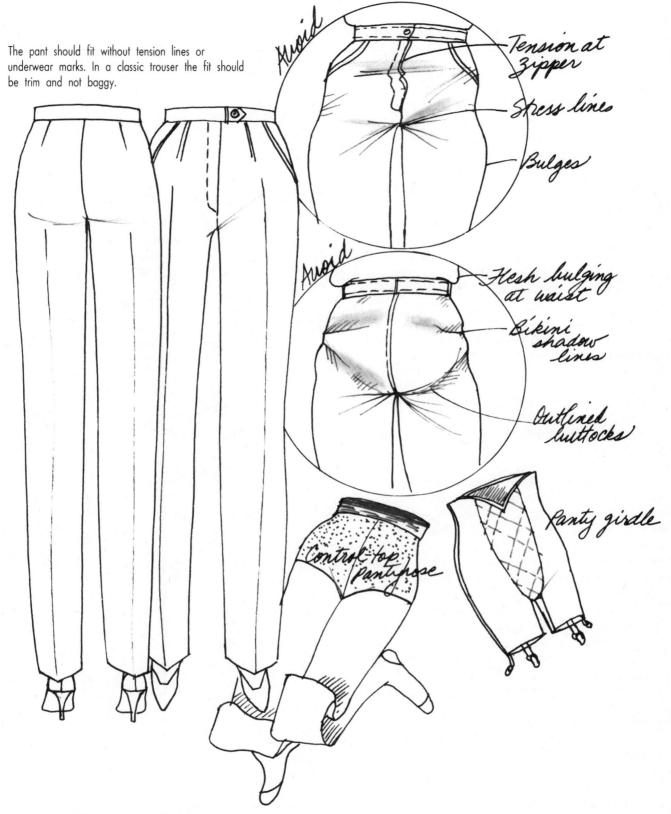

Avoid

Tension at zipper

Stress lines

Bulges

Avoid

Flesh bulging at waist

Bikini shadow lines

Outlined buttocks

Control-top pantyhose

Panty girdle

lightweight fabrics that demand a slip for modesty's sake. Often, these fabrics are so transparent that the undergarment is meant to be visible. Select a full slip or a teddy and half slip with a cut that fits well under the dress. The color that works best under most garments is a nude that matches your skin. Wear a strap-less bra so your shoulders do not look like a mass of straps. Make sure the lower half of the slip is opaque enough so there are no visible shadow lines from your underwear. Lace trim on slips and teddies can be attractive if it is compatible with the outer garments and is appropriately placed.

72

Proper Fit: Women

Minimum comfort ease for a fitted garment

2 inches

1 to 1½ inches

2 to 3 inches

CLOTHING FRAMES THE PERSONALITY and should not hinder or detract from a person's activities. Clothing should be comfortable. You should be able to relax in your clothes. Your clothing should allow you to perform the movements required by your job or activity.

Clothes that fit properly are vital. Wearing a size 10 when you are really a size 12 is the choice of an insecure woman. Garments that bulge at the bust and wrinkle at the hip declare, "I don't like my size 12 body and am trying to ignore it." Moreover, tight clothes accentuate figure problems. A gap at the bust line is a banner headline declaring that this is your major figure problem.

What is proper fit? Clothes that fit well flow smoothly over the body and do not cling or pull. There is ample ease over the contours of the body and room to move within the clothes without straining them.

The closure areas are particularly important when diagnosing proper fit. Zippers and button plackets are usually weaker than seams and fabric and therefore tend to gap or separate. When trying on clothes, first check the closures for tension lines. Then check to make sure there are no tension lines at the shoulders, bust, stomach, waist, and hip. The tension lines act like arrows directing attention to the problem area. Notice the stress placed on the fabric and hip line in the sketch on the previous page. Look at the difference between the two outfits on the facing page.

Typical *minimum* ease in a garment is 1 to 1½ inches at the waistline and 2 to 3 inches at the hips, so a person may sit comfortably. Two inches at the bust will allow for arm and torso movement. This is the least amount of fabric you should be able to pinch out of a garment you are wearing.

A professional singer once tried to claim a liberal clothing deduction from her income tax, stating that her evening gowns were a legitimate expense of business. It was disallowed. She retaliated by having her performing garments made so snug at the hipline she could wear them only standing up, to demonstrate that these clothes could be used for performing only and not for sitting and socializing. The clothes were declared deductible!

Stretch fabrics have revolutionized fit standards and fashions for many types of apparel. Because they

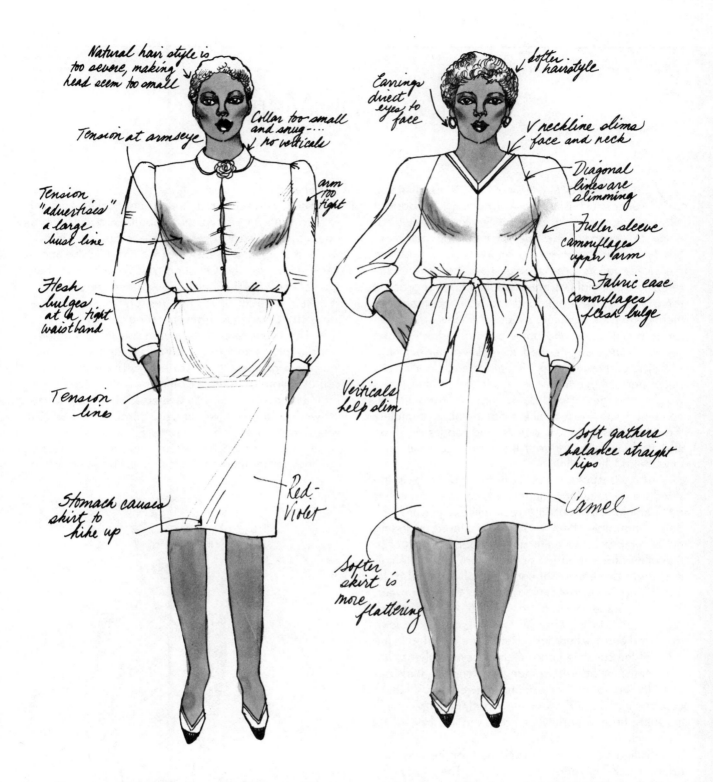

Natural hair style is too severe, making head seem too small

Tension at armseye

Tension "advertises" a large bust line

Flesh bulges at a tight waistband

Tension line

Stomach causes skirt to hike up

Collar too small and snug---- no verticals

arm too tight

Red-Violet

Earrings direct eyes to face

softer hairstyle

V neckline slims face and neck

Diagonal lines are slimming

Fuller sleeve camouflages upper arm

Fabric ease camouflages flesh bulge

Verticals help slim

Soft gathers balance straight hips

Camel

Softer skirt is more flattering

stretch so much, ease is not required. Lycra® is a stretch fiber that can be blended with many other types of fibers to create a wide range of fabrics. Garments made from such fabrics may fit snugly; but they are too tight if they force flesh to bulge or roll over at the waistline or hip line, or cause discomfort.

Fit is a function of fashion. The volume styled into clothing is often greater than the amounts for minimum comfort that we have just described. When a fashion cycle requires a full, softer silhouette, a lot of ease is added to garments. Proper fit of novelty garments is defined by fashion as well as by the physical demands of your activities.

73

Proper Fit: Men

THE FIT OF A FORMAL BUSINESS SUIT is essential to a successful business look. Tradition is the basis of all menswear fashion, and the Saville Row suit has come to epitomize the finest suit a man can own. Saville Row is the street in London where most fine menswear tailors are located. The "bespoken" suit refers to a suit that has been "spoken for," or ordered for a specific customer and made to his measurements. After the customer's measurements have been taken, a suit jacket and pants pattern is drafted, and several fittings are needed to make a perfect fit.

The custom-made suit should fit each individual's body perfectly, and may be altered if the man's weight changes. Hand-done inner construction is combined with fine machine-made details to complete the suit. Styles of lapels, details, and fabrics are flexible, and the tailor suggests the most successful combinations to his client.

The "bespoken," or custom-made suit, is the standard of excellence that ready-to-wear garments try to emulate. Even off-the-rack suits use construction details that allow them to be easily altered, including easily removed sleeve linings, waistband construction that allows for expansion or reduction, resettable collars, and side seams that can be easily tapered or let out. Sizing is more detailed than in women's wear. Suits are made in *short* (for men 5'8" and under), *regular* (5'8" to 6'), *long* (6' to 6'3"), and *extra long* (6'4" and over). Alterations usually are included in the price of the suit. Even casual pants commonly are left unhemmed or offered in many leg lengths. Shirts are sized to fit a variety of neck and sleeve sizes. All these construction details allow the garment to be more carefully fit to a variety of body shapes than is the case with women's wear.

Styling details also are selected for the way they adapt a jacket to various body shapes. The vents in the seat of a jacket were first used to allow the jacket to part over the legs of a man astride a horse. Vents allowed for freer movement and made pants pockets more accessible. Double-vented jackets are best suited to a tall, slender figure and should be avoided by men with wide hips or a prominent rear. A single vent makes a man seem slightly shorter, but does not call attention to a prominent derriere. A single vent is stylistically correct with a three-button jacket. A jacket with no vents is most typical of Continental styling and does not allow easy access to the pockets. It will bunch when seated, and is best worn by a tall, slim man. Vents should be short enough (7 to 9 inches) so they are not obvious. The jacket should have enough room in the hip area so there is no stress on the vent and the jacket falls smoothly from the shoulder line.

The same rules that govern the fit of women's wear apply to menswear. Wrinkles and stress lines indicate a garment that does not fit. These stress lines call attention to the part of the body they cover and should be avoided. Slightly oversized shirts emphasize the wedge-shaped torso, and are attractive, especially when worn with slender pants. Pants may be supported with suspenders, which require a waistband one inch larger than do pants that will be worn with a

Double Vent
Avoid if you have a prominent derriere

Single Vent
Most versatile style

No Vent
This baylord-Packer suit is best on tall, slim men

belt. When a man has a full stomach, suspenders act to anchor the pants at an appropriate waist height. Avoid wearing pants above or below a paunch. Have the waistband fit for an appropriate size, and select either belts or suspenders to secure the pants.

To determine if a garment fits properly, examine the rear view as carefully as you do the front of the garment. Utilize the advice of an expert tailor or sales-person. Be aware of figure imperfections like a low shoulder or extra-wide shoulders, and critically examine any garment you are buying, to see whether it can be altered to camouflage your figure imbalance. Remember that fit is essential to the success of both casual and formal business garments for men.

74

Fit for the Larger Woman

*T*HE LARGER WOMAN needs to define and slim her figure with vertical lines and not overwhelm it with flowing tunics and smocks. Too large a garment emphasizes the figure problem instead of minimizing it.

As a woman's girth increases, the length of her garments must also increase. The shoulders and bust are fuller and require more length to cover them. Evaluate the length of a top by bending over at the waist and checking to make sure there is no skin showing at the waistline. Avoid the overblouse that cuts the figure at mid-hip and reinforces the square silhouette.

The large woman should focus on the best attributes of her figure and dress to highlight them. The vertical line should be the theme of all garments. Clothes should fit the contours of the body, and stress lines should be carefully avoided. A slim silhouette should be created to minimize the bulk of the figure.

Thinner fabric, and more of it, will create the illusion of slimness. The fine texture and weight of the fabric will minimize bulk. Undergarments that are styled for opacity are the secret to the success of this look. Bulges that are visible through the sheer fabric will spoil the illusion.

Pants are not necessarily taboo for the larger woman. Pants must fit well to be effective. Avoid knits that are so soft they cling to the full thighs and stomach typical of the ample figure. Avoid elasticized waistbands that are the signature of pull-on pants. Instead, select pants that have a smooth waistband in the front and elastic in the back, or cover pull-on pants with an overblouse. The tailored waistband allows a blouse to be tucked in and still have the comfort of a stretch waistband. A straight pant leg or one with a very slight flare is the most flattering.

Picture Bea Arthur, the large, attractive woman from the television series "Maude" and "The Golden Girls." She is carefully dressed for the camera. Her successful formula is a soft blouse tucked into smooth pants or a slim or A-line skirt, covered with a three-quarter vest or slim tunic. This outfit is illustrated on the next page. Many variations are possible on this formula that stresses the vertical and successfully camouflages the derriere and the waist, two usual trouble spots for the large woman.

Too much fullness will make a large person seem even larger

Wear simple, understated jewelry

Keep hair away from neckline to slim silhouette

Coats are most effective if they are full length, that is, long enough to cover the skirts in your daytime wardrobe. A princess line and a flattering V neckline lead the eye to the face and emphasize length. Coats should be in a neutral or dark tone to look the slimmest.

Long skirts are flattering. If your legs are slim, use a side or front slit to emphasize the verticality of an outfit. Wear a jacket that comes to the upper hip area with a long skirt, and make sure the fabric is not too bulky. Avoid additional bulk by eliminating heavy sweaters, thick layers of outerwear jackets, and bulky furs.

Jewelry should focus attention on beautiful hands or a pretty face or handsome shoulders. Make sure the jewelry is large enough so it looks neither too small against the volume of the figure nor so large it exaggerates the body's size.

75

Fit: Tops and Sleeves

APPAREL MANUFACTURERS size garments specifically for the petite, average, and full-figured woman and for the different proportions of the junior and missy figure. But even within these general categories, fit varies widely. Every women's wear manufacturer has a different "ideal" type. By experimentation, find the manufacturer whose products fit you the best. Shop stores with a good selection of apparel that appeals to you and fits your figure type. If you have a problem figure, shop early in the season, because you will need a greater selection of garments than the average-size woman.

Carefully evaluate each top you purchase, especially if you are overweight. Clothing should be altered as little as possible, and tops, especially structured jackets, are the most difficult garments to alter.

The style and fit of a sleeve is the most important detail to attend to when selecting a top appropriate for your figure. A full sleeve camouflages an overweight arm, but too much fullness adds bulk to the arm and is unflattering. A sleeve that has a fuller armseye and that tapers to a slim wrist is an excellent way to visually slim the arm. The diagonal inset lines of a wedge-shaped raglan will minimize a full bust.

The traditional full kimono sleeve pictured at the top of the facing page creates few fit problems and successfully camouflages a full arm or ample bust. The tapered wrist is most flattering for the larger woman.

A set-in sleeve has a shoulder seam that joins the separate piece of fabric that forms the sleeve to the bodice. It is the most popular sleeve style. The set-in sleeve flatters the heavier figure if it fits properly. The armseye should not bind, and there should be ample ease around the upper arm. Large-size apparel must have unique patterns to accommodate the flesh that tends to accumulate on the upper arm and other parts of the body. Apparel that is graded (changing size in standard increments) from missy sizes will not fit the larger woman properly.

Beware of wearing a short sleeve that abruptly cuts the upper arm. This line broadens the look of a top on any but the slimmest figure. The bottom right-hand sketch on the facing page shows two ways to soften this line and make the arm seem thinner.

Sleeveless garments are difficult to wear when your upper arm is heavy or flabby. The cut of the armhole is important. A cap sleeve widens the shoulder. This is a flattering line if you need a broader shoulder to balance the width of your hips. The bottom right-hand examples on the facing page illustrate styles that camouflage a heavy upper arm effectively. Sleeveless garments are not appropriate for formal women's business wear, but cap sleeves are appropriate for warm-weather climates and under jackets.

Truly bare sleeveless garments are only effective on perfectly balanced shoulders. The abrupt armhole focuses attention on the width of the shoulders and the shape of the upper arm. The cutaway armhole makes narrow shoulders seem narrower because of the diagonal line of the bodice. Wide shoulders will seem even wider in this style by contrast with the small shoulder line.

Many tops are fitted with darts or *ease* (gathers, pleats, or extra fabric). Darts must fit the figure exactly to be effective. A dart should end slightly before the fullest part of the figure. The fullest part of the bust should be at least 1 inch above the end of the dart. Too sharp a dart line will form an awkward shape. Darts that fit improperly focus attention on the part of the anatomy that is poorly fit. Ease does not have to fit as precisely as darts and is an effective and easy way to shape fabric over a body's contours.

Sleeveless

Abrupt and unflattering unless arms are very slim.

Makes shoulders seem wider. Only for firm arms.

The traditional Kimono sleeve is too full at the wrist to flatter a large torso

A Kimono sleeve with a tapered wrist is more flattering

Unflattering set-in short sleeve

A cap sleeve is flattering for a full arm

Solutions

Novelty cap sleeve balances narrow shoulders

76

Construction: Tailored Jackets

*T*HE PURCHASE OF A JACKET or suit is usually a major financial commitment. You should evaluate the construction methods, details, and fit as well as the color and quality of the outer fabric. A well-tailored jacket feels good when you put it on. It hangs well on your body and has substance. A well-made jacket will last for many years, making the reward of wearing a finely tailored garment that is appropriate for many occasions well worth the investment. Remember, a $300 jacket you wear six or eight times a month is a better value than a less expensive jacket you wear only twice a year.

It is easier to judge the quality of a jacket if you know how it should be made. The most expensive tailored jackets are of wool, linen, or silk and are hand tailored. The interlining acts as a foundation for the shell (outer) fabric and is hand "padded" to shape the garment. *Padding* is the stitch that connects the interlining to the top fabric of the garment. Small, well-placed padding stitches reinforce the shape of the jacket. Shoulder pads add shape and allow the rest of the jacket to drape smoothly over the body. Additional handmade details include buttonholes, covered armseye seams, and hand-attached lining.

A tailored jacket can camouflage many figure problems, because it does not cling to the body when fitted properly. The jacket should fit the body smoothly, with no tension lines. The fabric is reinforced with interfacings so that body bulges are not visible. Perfect fit is the criterion of excellence in menswear. The finest women's wear is made to fit each individual body and is called *couture* in France, where designers still create these very expensive garments.

Many ready-to-wear garments substitute less expensive construction methods for the inner construction of couture and hand-tailored jackets. *Fusing* has been developed as an economical alternative to hand tailoring. Interfacings are coated with a thin layer of a gluelike substance and bonded to the jacket fabric with heat and pressure. A variety of weights and types of interfacings are available, so different weight fabrics may be accommodated.

Well-made garments have extensive interfacings fused to the body, lapel, and collar, depending on the weight of the fabric and the style of the jacket. A better

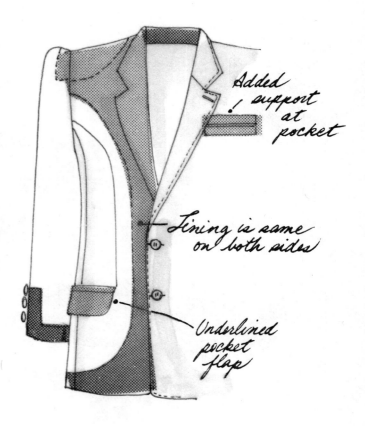

Added support at pocket

Lining is same on both sides

Underlined pocket flap

garment will have the same amount of fused interfacings as a hand-tailored garment has hand-padded interfacings. As a jacket increases in price and quality, the amount of fusing increases, because each piece that is fused adds to the cost of the garment.

Construction details are often hidden by the lining of a garment, and quality is difficult for the unpracticed eye to detect. Here are some ways to determine the quality of a garment. Flip up the back of the collar and see if small stitches are visible on the undercollar; these indicate hand tailoring. Observe the stand and firmness of the collar and the roll of the lapel: The softly curving roll of the front lapel should have no breaks or buckles; the lapel and collar should frame the face and be of a balanced and graceful size and proportion; the leading edge should be straight and very flat. It costs nothing to try on the most expensive garments in a store, so try on an expensive ready-to-wear garment and carefully evaluate the style,

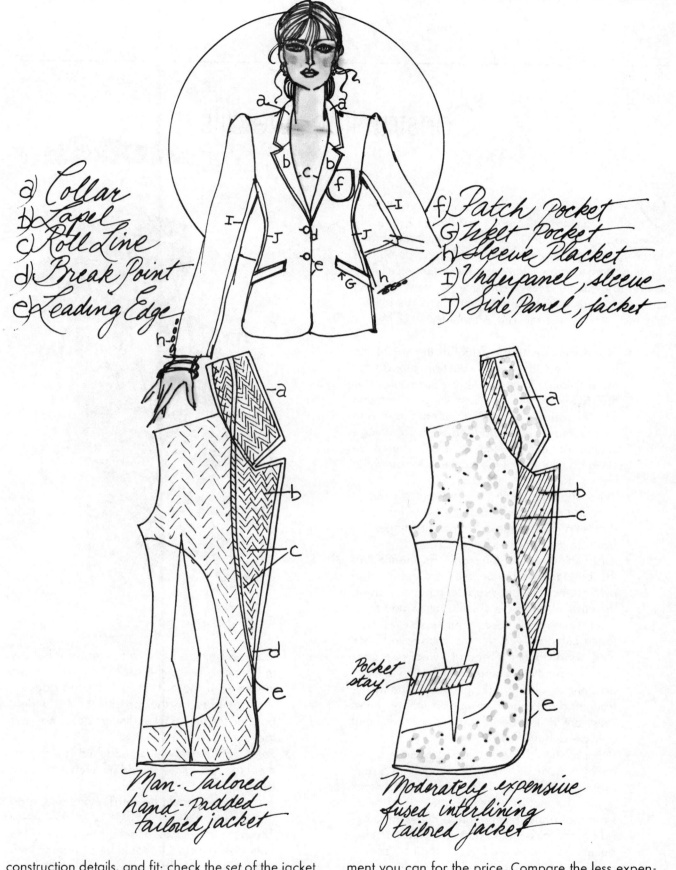

a) Collar
b) Lapel
c) Roll Line
d) Break Point
e) Leading Edge

f) Patch Pocket
G) Inset Pocket
h) Sleeve Placket
I) Underpanel, sleeve
J) Side Panel, jacket

Man-Tailored
hand-padded
tailored jacket

Moderately expensive
fused interlining
tailored jacket

Pocket stay

construction details, and fit; check the *set* of the jacket (the way the garment sits on your shoulders). Now try on jackets in your price range and compare them to the more expensive garments. Select the best gar-

ment you can for the price. Compare the less expensive garment's style, fit, and fabrication with those of the better jacket. Fine tailoring and good fabric are the mark of quality in a garment, not trendy styling.

77

Construction: Details

ETAILS ARE IMPORTANT indicators of quality in a tailored garment. Small parts that are perfectly sewn add up to a quality product. Your budget may force you to compromise on some of these points, but it is important to know what the standard of excellence is and to evaluate a less expensive garment to select the greatest value for your money. Look for the following things in a well-tailored garment:

- *Good shoulder pads* establish the set of the jacket. They should provide firm support for the shoulder line and be shaped to conform to the type of sleeves they support. Raglan sleeves require a softly rounded shape and set-in sleeves are padded with a wedge shape. An extra piece of fabric should be sewn into the top of the armseye to round the sleeve head.

- There should be *no hollow between the shoulders and the chest.* A smooth flow of fabric indicates a chest piece or fusing that shapes the front of the jacket.

- *All plackets should function.* This means that the buttons and buttonholes on sleeves and pockets should work. Napoleon put buttons on the cuffs of his soldiers' uniforms to stop them from wiping their noses on their sleeves. Buttoned cuffs allowed sleeves to be rolled back when working. Since ready-to-wear suits cannot have functional cuffs because they are impossible to alter, working cuffs became the trademark of a custom-made suit. The finest suits are still constructed with cuffs that can be unbuttoned.

- *Buttons* should be of good-quality bone, metal, wood, or shell. Plastic buttons easily break or chip. Buttons should have a shank made of metal or thread so they stand away from the fabric far enough to allow the other side of the jacket to be buttoned without being pulled or crushed. *Buttonholes* should be bound or have a rounded end with a well-stitched edge.

- *All pockets should work and be finished* with shell fabric on the inner side and lining on the top side. Lining is not visible when your hand is in the pocket, and the shell fabric will sustain the wear of the pocket as the hand goes in. Lining is used on the top side of the underpocket so the pocket lining does not get too thick.

- *Patch pockets* should be attached to the garment securely. They should be even if they are used in pairs.

- *Top stitching* should be small, even, and in an appropriate color.

- The *lining* should be attached by hand at the bottom of a jacket. It should be at least an inch shorter than the shell fabric and have a release fold at the hem to allow for movement. The lining should be finished around the edge of back vents. It should have a release pleat at

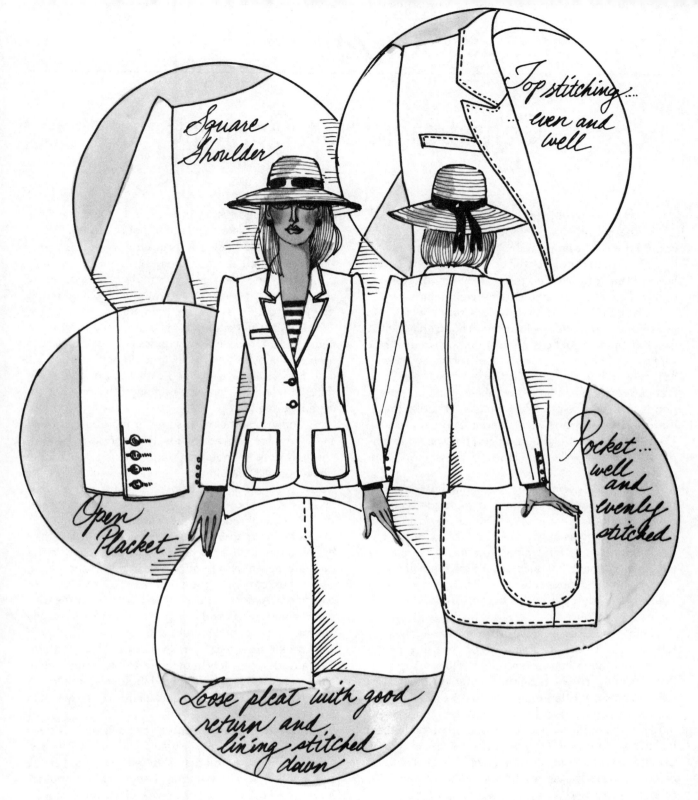

Square Shoulder

Top stitching... ...even and well

Open Placket

Pocket... well and evenly stitched

Loose pleat with good return and lining stitched down

the vertical center back seam to allow for shoulder movement.

▼ *An unlined jacket should look finished when taken off.* (A lightweight, spring/summer jacket, for instance, may be unlined.) The facings should be large enough to conceal shoulder pads and interfacings. Seams should be bound or finished to prevent raveling.

▼ A *lining* should be of good-quality fabric in a color compatible with the shell fabric. Beware of a very stiff or heavy lining, which may be there to give the shell fabric more body, indicating that the fabric is of inferior quality.

▼ Any *hidden snaps* on a jacket should be covered with a piece of lining fabric the same color as the jacket so there is no flash of metal.

78

Construction: Soft Garments

*E*XAMINE THE INTERIOR of a garment before you buy it. The construction methods tell you a great deal about how the garment will wear. Look at the seams first. They should not pucker or pull. They should be finished, because raw edges will ravel and look unsightly. The most common commercial method of finishing a seam is with a *sew overlock seam*, which is a cover stitch combined with a maching running stitch (see example 1). Knit garments usually have *overlock seams*, a finish that allows the fabric to stretch naturally without pulling stitches out (example 2). A *French seam* is a fine finish for lightweight, transparent goods, but it is expensive to make. It looks like a narrow tube of fabric at the seam line (example 3). The edges of lightweight fabric can be *pinked* (example 4), but this will often leave a press mark in a sheer fabric.

Fine men's garments have a seam that is *pressed open*. Casual pants have a *welt seam*, made by using a sew overlock seam and adding an extra stitch to hold the edge of the seam down against the outer fabric. A *flat-felled seam*, typical of jeans, is created by cutting one seam allowance wider than the other, lapping it over the shorter side, and stitching it down. This finish is quite durable and is particularly appropriate for heavy cottons.

Flat-felled seams also are used for lightweight fabrics, which do not require great care in pressing and so can have their seam edges stitched together. Because they create a finished inner garment, flat-felled seams are often found on men's shirts. Heavier fabrics, typically used for tailored skirts and pants, must have the seams pressed flat and open for the best look. The edges of the seams may be overlocked (see example 5), which stops raveling with the least amount of added bulk. The edges can be hemmed (example 6), but an extra ridge is produced that can be visible after the garment has been pressed. The seams can be edged with a thin seam tape (example 7), a method employed most often in European garments. Edge finishing is expensive, because the seam has to be handled three times instead of the one that sew overlock requires, and then seamed sections of the garment must be taken out of the sewing machine to be underpressed (seam pressed opened) before the garment is completed and has its final pressing. Pinked seams (example 8) stop raveling but will leave a zigzag mark when pressed over.

Check the cuff finish of a shirt or a dress. A raw edge at the cuff prevents you from turning it up and is a sign of a less expensive garment.

Lining is necessary for pants and skirts made in heavy or textured woolens. Fabrics that have blends of fibers that may irritate the skin should be lined. Fabrics that are loosely woven, such as tweeds and flannels, should be lined, to prevent bagging after one has sat in the garments.

Apply to soft clothes some of the quality guidelines given for tailored jackets. Look for good buttons, carefully dyed to match or blend with the shell fabric. Check top stitching, to make sure it is even. A dress or blouse with light shoulder pads will hang well on your body, and the shoulder pads will prevent hanger wear.

Remove thread belt loops from dresses immediately after purchasing the garment. They are added by the manufacturer to keep the belt attached to the garment and may hit your body at the wrong place. Do not hesitate to upgrade a belt or buttons if you like a garment. A manufacturer often has to cut corners on these accessories, and the garment may be greatly enhanced by a better belt.

Make sure that sportswear tops and bottoms purchased separately match. Dye lots of the same color can vary slightly. To avoid this problem, a manufacturer should ship garments all from one dye lot to a store.

Carefully examine fabrics for flaws such as slubs (a thick bump on a yarn), holes, and pulled threads. Some fabrics are naturally slubbed as a part of the surface design of the fabric. Usually, the manufacturer's descriptive hang tag will alert the customer when such is the case.

1. Sew Overlock Seam

3. French Seam

2. Overlock Seam

4. Pinked Seam

5.

6.

7.

8.

Inside-out view of well-tailored trousers with menswear detailing

79

Accessories: Shoes

THE WORD *SHOE* should be followed immediately by the word *comfort*. A shoe, no matter how spectacular the style, is worthless if it does not fit. Limping along or being hampered by impractical styles is pure folly. Uncomfortable shoes spoil your carriage and confidence. There are several guidelines about buying women's shoes that will ensure they are attractive and suited to your wardrobe.

1. *Avoid heavy shoes.* A clunky shoe makes thin legs look like toothpicks and exaggerates the bulk of heavy legs.

2. *A medium heel makes you appear taller* and nearer the fashion height ideal of eight head lengths. The legs seem more attractive, because the instep of the foot has a graceful arch and the slight contraction of the calf muscle caused by the raised heel gives the calf better shape.

3. *A contrasting color,* whether bright, light, or very dark, *focuses attention on the feet.* This interrupts a unified line and tends to make a person seem shorter. When buying a contrasting shoe, ask yourself if you want your audience to look first at your feet.

4. *Shoes do not have to match your garments;* they can blend or be in a tone that relates to your wardrobe. Models usually carry a neutral shoe, the color of their skin, to wear with unusual colors.

5. *The closer the shoe color to your leg color and the simpler the style, the slimmer and more graceful your legs will seem.*

6. *Balance the kind of shoe with the kind of garment.* Do not team a heavy shoe with a soft dress or a dressy shoe with a serious wool tweed suit.

7. *Select boot styles with tops tall enough to be covered by the hem of the skirt.* Do not allow a sliver of leg to show. Boots are wonderfully practical for cold, wet weather. Wet weather demands a practical, all-weather boot. Carry a spare pair of shoes to wear in the office and on rainy days.

Shoes cost a great deal, but you do not need to have an extensive wardrobe to dress your feet in style. Consider buying several basic shoes in neutral colors suited to your palette. Wear them until they are no longer presentable, and then replace them. It is not necessary to match shoes to a garment.

Experiment with shoes for your casual wardrobe. Often you can purchase inexpensive casual shoes. A casual loafer is a good bet for jeans and casual pants. Espadrilles, simple sandals, and classic favorites like the Chinese canvas Mary-Jane are appealing with casual clothes. The final word for shoe selection should be simplicity. Avoid ankle straps that shorten the visual length of the leg. Ornaments that are sewn or glued on have a greater chance of falling off and spoiling the shoe's looks.

Men's formal business shoes should be darker than the suit. This rule of thumb makes black shoes correct with all other colors, especially navy and grey. Brown shoes are more casual. The classic men's shoe style is the brogue, or wingtip. The brogue originated in Scotland as a heavy work shoe pierced with holes to let bog water pass in and out of the shoe. These were formalized into the American wingtip with decorative holes. Semibrogues have only a toe-cap with holes. Oxfords, a basic, front-lacing shoe cut below the ankle, are appropriate for all suits. The loafer has been adapted to business wear by the Italians, and is now appropriate for formal and informal business

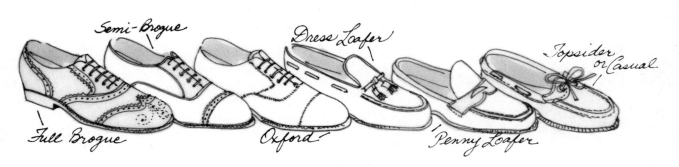

Semi-Brogue · Dress Loafer · Topsider or Casual

Full Brogue · Oxford · Penny Loafer

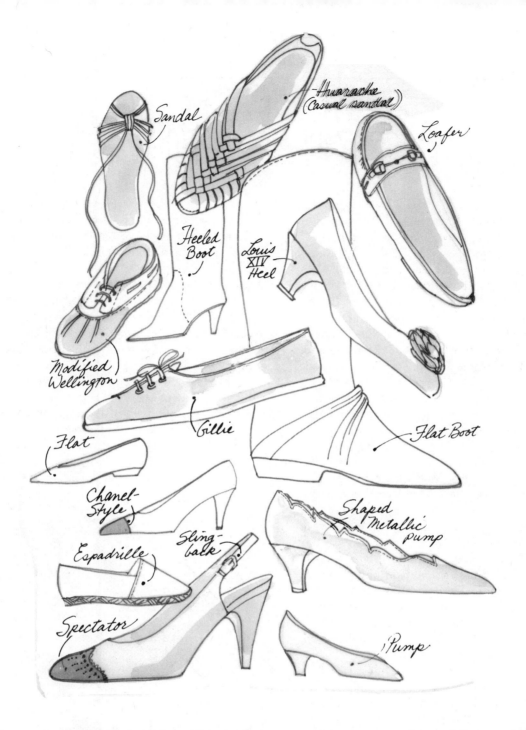

Sandal

Huarache
(Casual sandal)

Loafer

Heeled
Boot

Louis
XIV
Heel

Modified
Wellington

Gillie

Flat Boot

Flat

Chanel-
Style

Shaped
Metallic
pump

Espadrille

Sling-
back

Spectator

Pump

wear. More casual styles include the penny loafer, introduced by Bass Weejuns in the 1930s and a classic today. Boat shoes and canvas active wear complete the casual shoe spectrum.

Boots were popular for formal menswear until the eighteenth century. Work boots are an essential part of the wardrobe of many men in physical occupations. They lend support to the ankle, add traction, and protect the foot. Some men enjoy wearing boots of all types for casual wear. The cowboy boot has become a classic.

Working people spend many hours on their feet and should pay special attention to their shoe

purchases. A second pair of shoes to change to during a long day will reduce foot fatigue. This is a must if you are on vacation and walking a great deal. Women should beware of high heels that look wonderful but are uncomfortable and abuse the feet and legs.

Keep shoes in excellent repair. A little care can renew dirty or scuffed shoes. Use fine saddle soap and excellent leather preparations to keep your shoes looking their best. For wet weather, water repellants such as mink oil will condition the leather soles as well as the tops. The shoemaker can do wonders in repairing run-down heels and soles to extend the life of a pair of shoes.

Accessories: Stockings

THE MOST VERSATILE STOCKING for women is a natural skin tone, with a nude toe and no heel reinforcement. This stocking will slip into any shoe, work with any garment, and blend into the complete outfit easily. Natural hose is a good basic for serious business clothes. Black women should select a tone that blends with and is a shade darker than their skin tone. A shade that is close to natural but does not quite make it has a strange look that should be avoided.

Colored hose create some interesting illusions. The trick in selecting novelty hose is to balance the leg interest with the texture, color, and weight of your outfit. Generally, if you are wearing a dark bottom made from heavier-weight fabric, you can wear a stocking in a subtle tone of the skirt. This adds to the illusion of height, especially when the shoe is in the same color.

Lighter-colored clothes and clothes in delicate fabrics look handsome with light-colored hose and a light shoe. Do not wear white stockings with bone or beige shoes; the shades are just enough off to seem like a mistake. Avoid combining very dark shoes with off-white hose, unless you are trying for an "Alice in Wonderland" look. This combination highlights the legs.

Avoid wearing exotic-colored stockings when dressing for a serious business occasion. Florid pink, red, or purple hose give your legs a very peculiar look. Your audience will notice your legs before they hazard a glance at your face.

Businessmen should wear hose that match their shoe color and are long enough to cover the calf so bare leg does not show when the pant leg is raised. Elasticized hose solve the problem of keeping the socks up. Men's casual wear socks may be in bright colors or patterns that accent the colors of the outfit. White athletic socks are a classic appropriately worn with tennis and other casual shoe styles. Socks with a high cotton or wool (for winter) fiber content are the most comfortable, because they are resilient, cushion the foot, and absorb perspiration.

Women's socks and stockings also can be selected for whimsical effects, especially with casual clothes. Argyle socks can be worn by both men and women to tie together the patterns and colors in a flannel sporting outfit. Are you tall and slender and able to carry a fashion effect? Wear a brightly con-

trasting sock under your neutral pants and team it with a sporty tie or novelty vest in the same accent color. Socks are practical comfort accessories, especially in cold and wet weather. One or two layers cushion an abrasive boot and provide warmth.

Tights are heavier versions of panty hose. They are comfortable during cold weather for insulating women's legs under pants and skirts. They are very handsome teamed with garments that have weight and texture.

The perennial basic is the nude leg look, appropriate for all occasions. Real zing can be added to an outfit with the right novelty stocking if it suits your figure type and leg shape. Let the mirror be your guide. Avoid too radical an effect, especially for business.

Experiment with this inexpensive and versatile accessory to enhance your figure and outfit.

Patterned hose make an elegant accessory for evening clothes

Accessories: Handbags, Briefcases, and Wallets

*H*ANDBAGS AND BRIEFCASES complete the picture of a formal businessperson and are necessary to carry papers and other personal items. Quality accessories are vital. Leather is the most versatile material and is shaped and styled into a great variety of carrying cases. The two basic types are the structured bag and the limp, or unstructured bag. *Structured bags* have a stiff frame with a covering stretched over it. Ordinarily, smooth, lightweight leathers are used to cover the frame, because they are reinforced by the foundation. *Unstructured bags* frequently are made from thicker, grained leather. These leathers must be more durable, and often are easier to saddle soap and clean, though they usually are less formal than the structured bag. Quality findings, handles, hinges, and locks are the components of a fine handbag. Exotic leathers, like reptile, alligator, and ostrich, are expensive and are not essential for a quality bag. A good-quality leather bag, well designed, kept in excellent repair, and in a color that blends with a person's total wardrobe, is an accessory investment that will last for several seasons if chosen with care.

Women who lead busy lives have little time to deal with "time-eaters" like shifting possessions from handbag to handbag. This chore can be eliminated by selecting a bag that is appropriate for most daytime activities. Blend it with your shoe wardrobe (fashion no longer decrees that shoes and bags match) and your basic wardrobe colors, and use a daytime bag day after day. Purchase an excellent-quality purse, because your handbag is a highly visible part of your total look and will definitely detract from your appearance if it is obviously inexpensive, worn out, or inappropriate. Leather-lined bags wear best. A cloth lining will wear out before the shell does. Suede and cloth bags tend to get dirty sooner than quality leathers.

Avoid toting around a huge purse loaded with all the gimcracks that have accumulated in it since its purchase. Businesswomen should avoid this "saddle bag," because it detracts from an efficient, professional appearance. Go through your purse now and look at all the things that have collected there. Eliminate the junk. Evaluate the makeup you carry—you probably have too much. Consolidate your credit cards and money into one simple wallet. Carry a notepad with pencil or pen attached. Make sure all your keys are on one simple ring. Separate the absolutely essential things to carry in your bag. Purchase an organizer or a slim briefcase in which to carry your papers and business equipment.

Men and women should select a bag by fitting all of their necessary equipment in it before buying it. Make sure it is not distorted by what you want to carry, and that is closes easily. Check the handle and strap, to make sure it is attached securely—it will take the most stress. The clasp should be secure, to discourage losses and theft.

Drawstring Saddle-bag

Tote

Satchel

Tailored Saddle bag

Quilted Chanel

Reptile clutch

Novelty "hatbox" shape

Clutch

Minaudière

Women may wish to select two bags to use during the year—one for lighter-weight and colored warm-weather clothing and another for winter clothes. Dressy evening clothes will require another bag. This can be a small, light pouch or clutch that blends with your evening clothes.

A handbag can point to a figure problem. Too large a bag will overwhelm a petite person. A brightly colored handbag detracts from the unity of an outfit coordinated to maximize height. A solid color purse in the same tonal family would be more appropriate. Either a very small bag or a very large one will emphasize the bulk of a large woman. A medium handbag would be less conspicuous.

Select quality leather accessories. A tacky wallet that is falling apart or bulging with too many cards and papers is a poor advertisement for a chic person. A quality wallet lasts for many years, so do not skimp on something that will reflect on your personal image every time you open your bag.

Accessories: Jewelry

EWELRY MAKES a personal statement. The kind and amount you wear says a great deal about your taste. The businessperson should pay particular attention to jewelry, for it is often a status symbol evaluated by others.

A safe rule to follow when selecting jewelry, particularly for men, is "less is more." Think of jewelry as providing the final accent for your outfit. Classic jewelry for men includes the signet or wedding ring, cufflinks (for French cuffs only), tie tacks and bars, tie clips (for narrow ties), and shirt studs for formal wear. Watches were developed from women's wear during World War I, because the traditional pocket watch was not functional in the trenches. The prosperous Victorian man thought it vulgar to be concerned with time, but the practicalities of business have banished that prejudice. Cartier developed the tank watch in 1917 for Brazilian aviator Santos-Durmot, and the style became a classic. The Rolex Perpetual (1930) was the first practical self-winding watch. Accuracy and durability defined fine watches until the invention of

quartz movements. The ring and watch remain the only men's jewelry correctly worn near the skin.

Businesswomen should avoid jewelry that clanks or seems too clunky. Jewelry should be the subtle accent that highlights a woman's good looks. Lustrous pearls at the neck and ears highlight a woman's coloring by contrasting with the skin. The subtle sparkle of trim earrings or a simple necklace dresses the basic business outfit and makes it seem finished. A suggestion of sparkle is the touch that balances dramatic evening makeup and a dramatic evening outfit.

Do not slavishly follow fashion photographs. Photographic stylists often exaggerate accessories, because the camera reduces the impact of subtle details. A high-fashion designer often accessorizes with extra bold jewelry to make clothes "read" from the runway. The customer would not like to duplicate the look. I remember seeing stunning, large "silver" jewelry worn on heavy winter clothes in a *prêt-à-porter* (ready-to-wear) collection show in Paris. When I went backstage to examine the clothes close up, I

Jewelry is too small   *Too much jewelry*   *Tasteful selection*

was amazed to discover that the jewelry had been made by cutting aluminum pie tins in shreds, bending them into interesting shapes, and tying them on with black ribbon!

Women should start selecting jewelry from the head down. Earrings are very important, because they highlight the face. Clip-on earrings can be annoying and cause headaches. Consider having your ears pierced for comfort and to prevent the loss of really valuable earrings.

Next move to your neck as a focal point. A woman with a large bust should not call attention to the obvious by wearing large, dangling pendants. Focus attention upward by wearing jewelry that is closer to the base of the neck. Avoid wearing a choker if your neck is short or heavy.

Very large women should focus attention on the hands and face. Carefully evaluate any body jewelry before wearing it. Too small a piece may emphasize your girth, while a very large piece may make you seem overwhelming. Small women too should carefully scale jewelry to their size.

Your color palette will suggest the stones and metals that are most flattering to you and that will blend best with your wardrobe. Gold and warm-toned metals are naturals for sunlight complexions, though antique silver is also handsome, especially when combined with ivory or warm-colored stones like turquoise. Moon glow complexions look beautiful in white metals. Diamonds are attractive on everyone, because they reflect light, but a mounting in a cool or warm-colored metal to compliment a person's palette will be most flattering.

83

Accessories: Belts

*B*ELTS ARE A WONDERFULLY VERSATILE accessory for the woman with a waist and hip line that can be highlighted. This lucky person can select exotic colors and sizes and include large buckles and dangly accessories.

Unusual belts are available from many sources other than the conventional store counter. Twist two contrasting scarves and tie them over a basic blouse or dress to achieve an original look for casual or at-home wear. Antique fabrics, ethnic ties, leather straps, or other found objects make attractive accessories. Belts are wonderful "collector's items" that can represent the many different places and people with which you have come in contact.

The woman with a figure problem must invest more time and thought in selecting a belt. Waistline definition can help to make her look slimmer. The trick to remember when belting a large figure is to make the belt as close to the color of the garment as possible. Remember all of the experiments on earlier pages—coloring belts in dark colors, advancing colors, and blending colors? The figure that did not have a contrasting horizontal division seemed the tallest and slimmest.

Tailored, slim belts should be a part of every woman's wardrobe. These are narrow enough to slip into belt loops and add a finish to the waistline of a tailored pant or skirt. The large woman should select blending colors and buckles that are made of oxidized (darkened) metal or self-covered in the belt material.

A belt with long ends will provide a slimming vertical. A belt should never be so wide or tight that it causes flesh to collect in a roll above it.

Men's belts for formal business wear should be leather in a shade darker than the pants. For casual wear, lighter leather belts may be worn. Casual belts in webbing or elastic also are appropriate and add interesting contrasts to many outfits.

An interesting alternative to a belt is a pair of braces, or suspenders. Braces were high fashion throughout the eighteenth and nineteenth centuries. Classic braces button to the .pants in front and back and are adjustable. They often are made with decorative webbing, and have an elegant look. They are comfortable because they hold pants in place without constricting the waist. They are cooler, as well as being a fashionable alternative to belts for men.

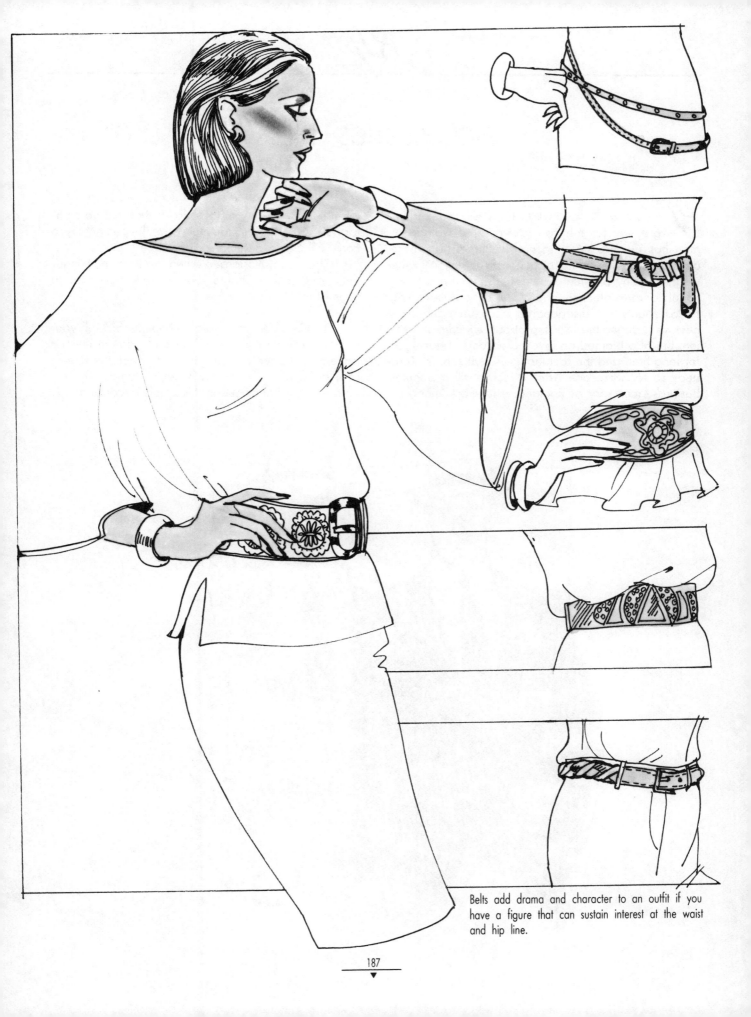

Belts add drama and character to an outfit if you
have a figure that can sustain interest at the waist
and hip line.

84

Accessories: Hats

THE DAY WHEN A TAILORED HAT was a required ingredient for the correctly dressed woman or man has passed. Wearing nonfunctional hats these days usually stirs comment and calls attention to the wearer. Many physical occupations require a functional hat for protection, and style is not a determining factor. Men's hats disappeared from American business wear during the 1960s, probably a victim of fashion, but also blamed on low-roofed cars, the fashion for long hair, and the fact that President John F. Kennedy rarely wore one. The bowler is still a popular business accessory in England. The most important requisite for wearing a hat today is that you be comfortable wearing one. You must have the personality to carry off being definitely different.

The visual illusions created by hats may influence your choice, should you decide to add a hat to your outfit.

1. *Consider your total silhouette first.* If your head is large for the size of your body, do not select a large hat. A closely fitted hat will balance the size of your head with your body. A petite woman wearing an overlarge hat or one that is boldly decorated may

Hat of same tone adds height

Beret

Sou'westerner

Turban

Scarf

Cloth

Jockey

Cowboy

Panama

Baseball

Straw

Boater

look like an elaborate mushroom The small woman generally should select tailored hats with modest brims and crowns.

2. *A hat that blends with an outfit carries the eye upward* and makes the person seem taller. A contrasting hat makes a person seem shorter.

3. *A hat with a slightly raised crown tends to make a person look taller.* It must not be too tall, or a short person will look dwarfed by the volume of the hat.

4. *A hat that sits squarely on top of the head makes the face seem fuller.* This can be used to advantage for the person with a very thin face. A hat tilted at an angle creates a diagonal and more slimming line.

5. *A hat should fit very well.* Too snug a hat will cause some discomfort and perhaps even a headache. Too loose a hat will slip and make the person appear comical. Hats can be tightened by stitching grosgrain ribbon into the inner band and slightly padding the hatband.

6. *The hair should be worn simply*, in a way that does not conflict with the size and flare of the hat. Women can slick back short hair or pull long hair into a knot or pony tail for a sleek, elegant look.

Hats are functional as well as decorative. Women can carry a soft-wrap hat or a beret in a coat pocket for protection on a rainy day. Hats to protect the face and head from the sun are an important outdoor accessory. Consider wearing a cowboy hat or a pith helmet for casual, sunny occasions. A visor secured on an elasticized head band or a soft cap is an excellent sun hat for active wear. A scarf can be fashioned into a hat and is the perfect travel accessory.

85

Accessories: Scarves and Ties

*S*CARVES ARE A WONDERFUL WAY to focus the eye on a specific part of a woman's body. A contrasting color can highlight the face by draping the scarf around the neck. Scarves can neutralize harsh clothing colors by adding a spot of your most flattering color close to the face. Contrasting scarves at the neckline of an open blouse emphasize the flattering V diagonals of the opening. A scarf makes a fine belt, or even a sexy bare top.

Wrap your head in a scarf when your hair is less than presentable. Drape a large wool or silk scarf over the shoulders of a jacket or coat for added warmth and color. Use a lace hankie tucked into the pocket of a tailored suit to soften the suit. Wear a long, narrow scarf knotted at the ends to provide slimming vertical lines. Use a bandana tied with a perky knot as a colorful sweatband when jogging or for other active sports. Notice how scarves are displayed in retail stores, and practice tying them several times to perfect the technique. Always have a clean and pressed scarf, because it will attract attention immediately if it is unkempt.

Men's ties evolved from the cravat of the seventeenth century. When an English school student took the striped band from his straw boater and tied it around his neck, the old school tie was born. The school stripe and foulard, a small woven pattern, remain two of the most important traditional patterns for men's ties. Dots are another favorite, with smaller dots more formal than larger ones. Trendy pattens, like paisleys and plaids, are popular variations.

Fine ties are cut on the bias, which helps them to tie smoothly. Silk ties are the most formal and are appropriate for all business situations. More casual knit ties, woven cottons, and novelties are appropriate for informal social and business situations. Select the size knot appropriate for the size of the shirt collar, face size, and size of the tie. A four-in-hand knot is slightly smaller than a Windsor, and is the most versatile tie knot. A Windsor knot balances a large face and a wide-spread collar. The wrinkles will fall out of a well-made tie if it is hung overnight. Of course, cleanliness is essential, so clean ties frequently.

Selecting a pattern tie and a color tie for each shirt-and-suit combination is a challenge, and the way a man can distinguish himself. Accent colors compli-ment personal coloring, and accent the neutral palette of typical business suits. Fashion often emphasizes a particular color or pattern, but a blending of colors is always acceptable using the classic accents—red, yellow, and blue. Dot or spot patterns are versatile accents with striped shirts. Solid-color ties are formal and are excellent when worn with a patterned shirt and suit. Remember the rule of thumb to combine two patterns and a solid when pulling together an outfit. A

boldly patterned shirt is most attractive with a solid color or simple, bold pattern as a compliment. A solid-color pastel shirt can carry a more subtle, complicated patterned or textured tie. Personal taste is the guideline in tie selection, but evaluate combinations you see in fine menswear stores and magazines to keep your personal statement current.

Handkerchiefs are an essential menswear accessory. A crisp linen or cotton square with a hand-rolled edge is the standard of excellence. There are several ways of folding the handkerchief: the simple flat fold, the multipointed fold, the triangle, and the puff. All are correct with formal business suits and are appropriate for more casual wear. Select a clean handkerchief each day. Colored squares are popular accents. The classic formal business pattern is the paisley, which should be worn with the puff fold only. Matching the pocket square to the tie looks very commercial.

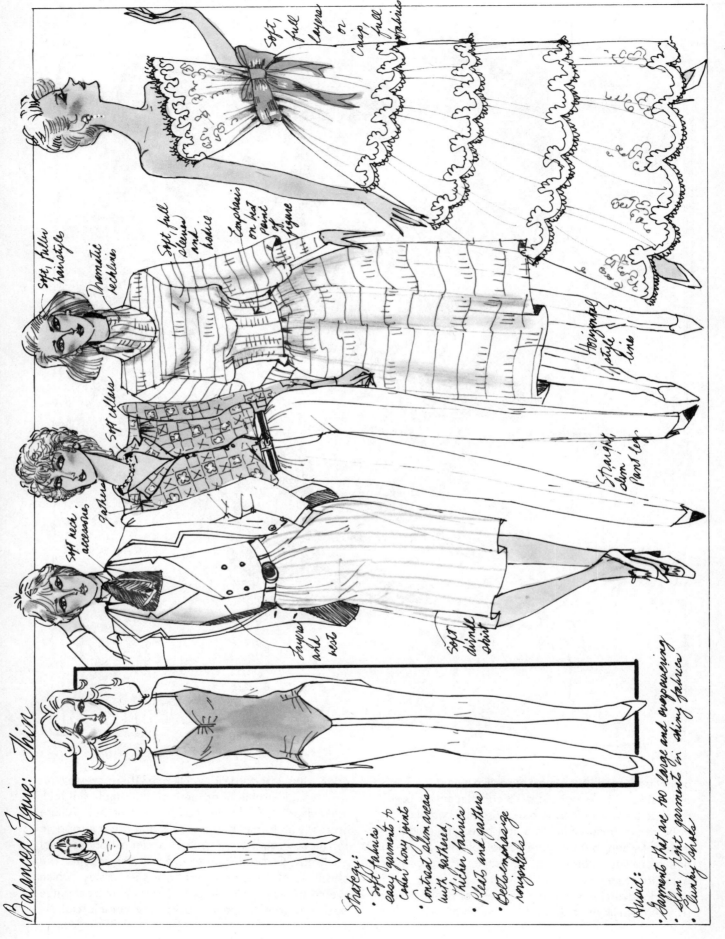

Balanced Figure: Thin

Soft, full cape or crop.

Soft, full neckline.

Soft, fuller hairstyle

Dramatic neckline

Soft, full sleeves and bodice

Emphasis on that point of figure

Soft collar

Horizontal style line

Straight, slim pant leg

Soft neck accessory

Gathering

Soft dirndle skirt

Strategy:
• Soft fabrics in easy garments to cover bony joints
• Contrast slim areas with gathered, thicker fabrics
• Pleat and gathers
• De-emphasize nonvertals

Avoid:
• Garments that are too large and overpowering
• Slim tight garments in shiny fabrics
• Clunky shoes

192
▼

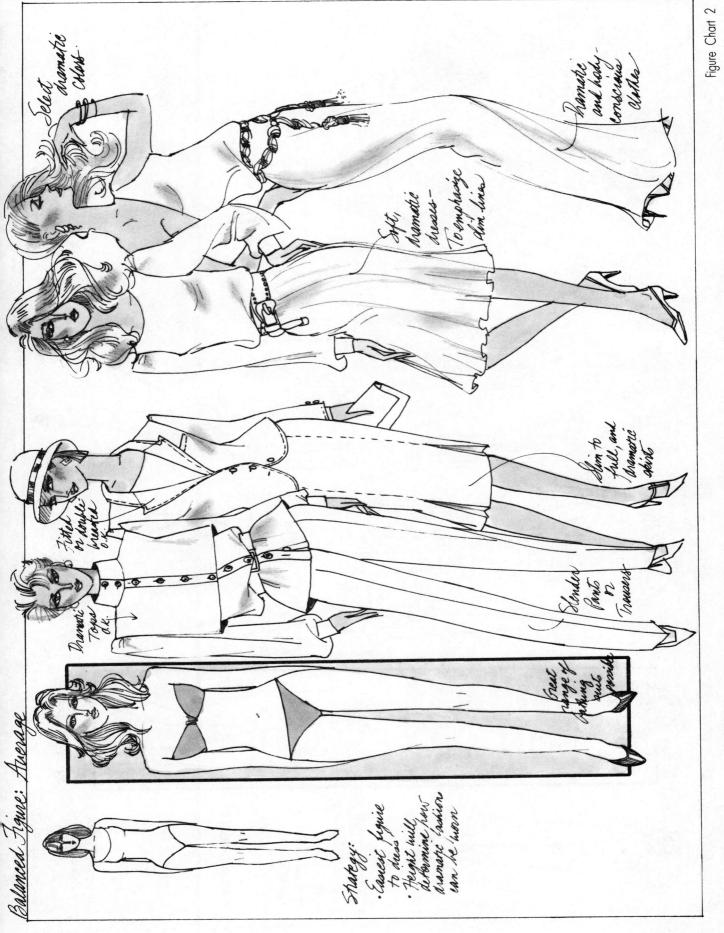

Balanced Figure: Average

Select dramatic colors

Dramatic and body-conscious clothes

Soft, dramatic dresses — to emphasize arm line

Slim to full, and dramatic skirts

Fitted or double-breasted O.k.

Dramatic tops O.k.

Slender pants or trousers

Great range of clothing will provide

Strategy:
• Earnest figure to dress
• Height will determine how dramatic fashion can be worn

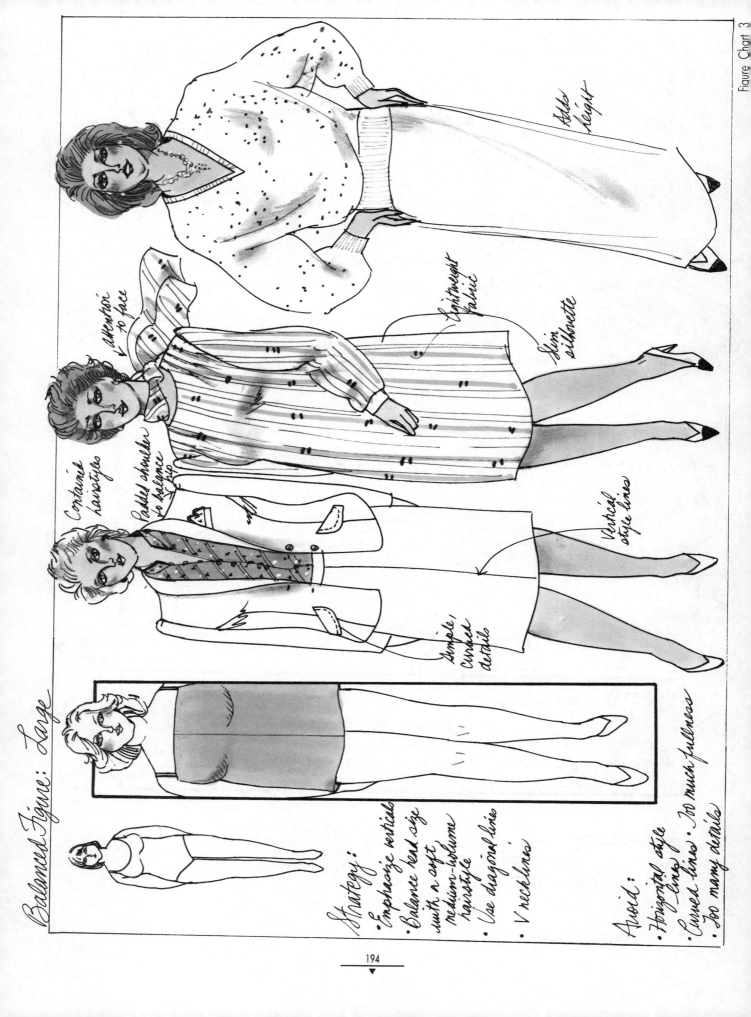

Balanced Figure: Large

Halo height

attention to face

Lightweight fabric

Slim silhouette

Contained hairstyle

Padded shoulder to balance hip

Simple, curved details

Vertical style lines

Strategy:
· Emphasize verticals
· Balance head size with a soft medium-volume hairstyle
· Use diagonal lines
· V neckline

Avoid:
· Horizontal style lines
· Curved lines · Too much fullness
· Too many details

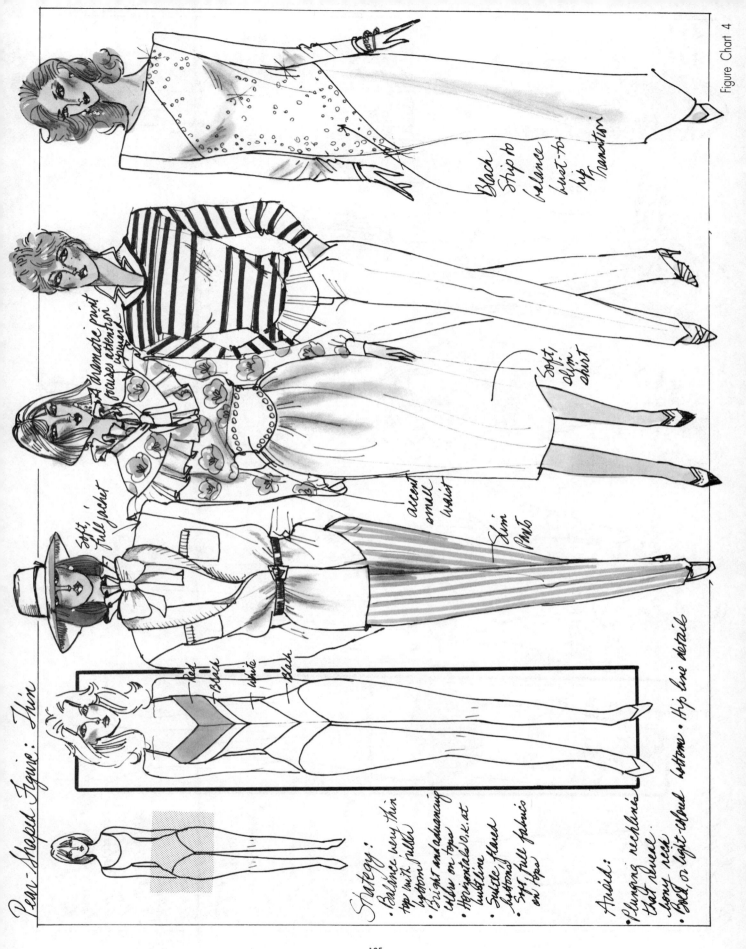

Pear-Shaped Figure: Thin

Black
Strip to
balance
bust-to-
hip
transition

A dramatic print
blouse attention
upward

Soft,
slim
shirt

Soft,
full jacket

accent
small
waist

Slim
Pants

Red
Black
White
Black

Strategy:
• Balance very thin
  top with fuller,
  bottom, fuller
• Bright and advancing
  color on top
• Horizontals o.k. at
  waistline
• Subtle, flared
  bottoms
• Soft, full fabric
  on hips

Avoid:
• Plunging neckline
  that reveal
  bony neck
• Bold, or light colored
  bottoms • Hip line details

Figure Chart 4

Pear-Shaped Figure: Average

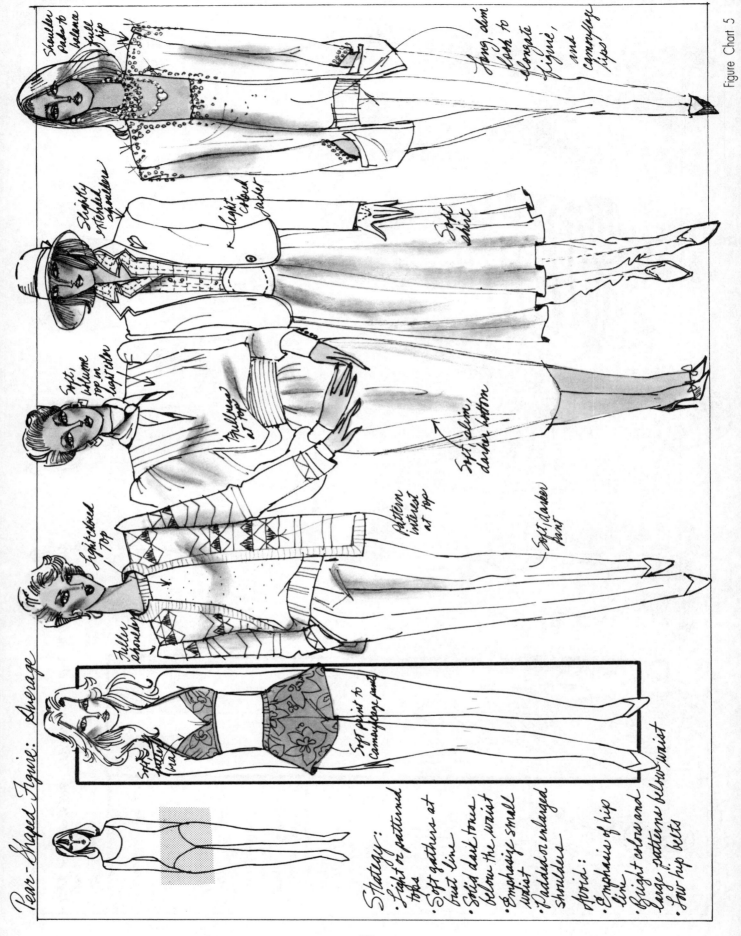

Strategy:
- Light or patterned tops
- Soft gathers at bust line
- Solid dark tone below the waist
- Emphasize small waist
- Padded or enlarged shoulders

Avoid:
- Emphasis of hip line
- Bright colors and large patterns below waist
- Low hip belts

Pear-Shaped Figure: Large

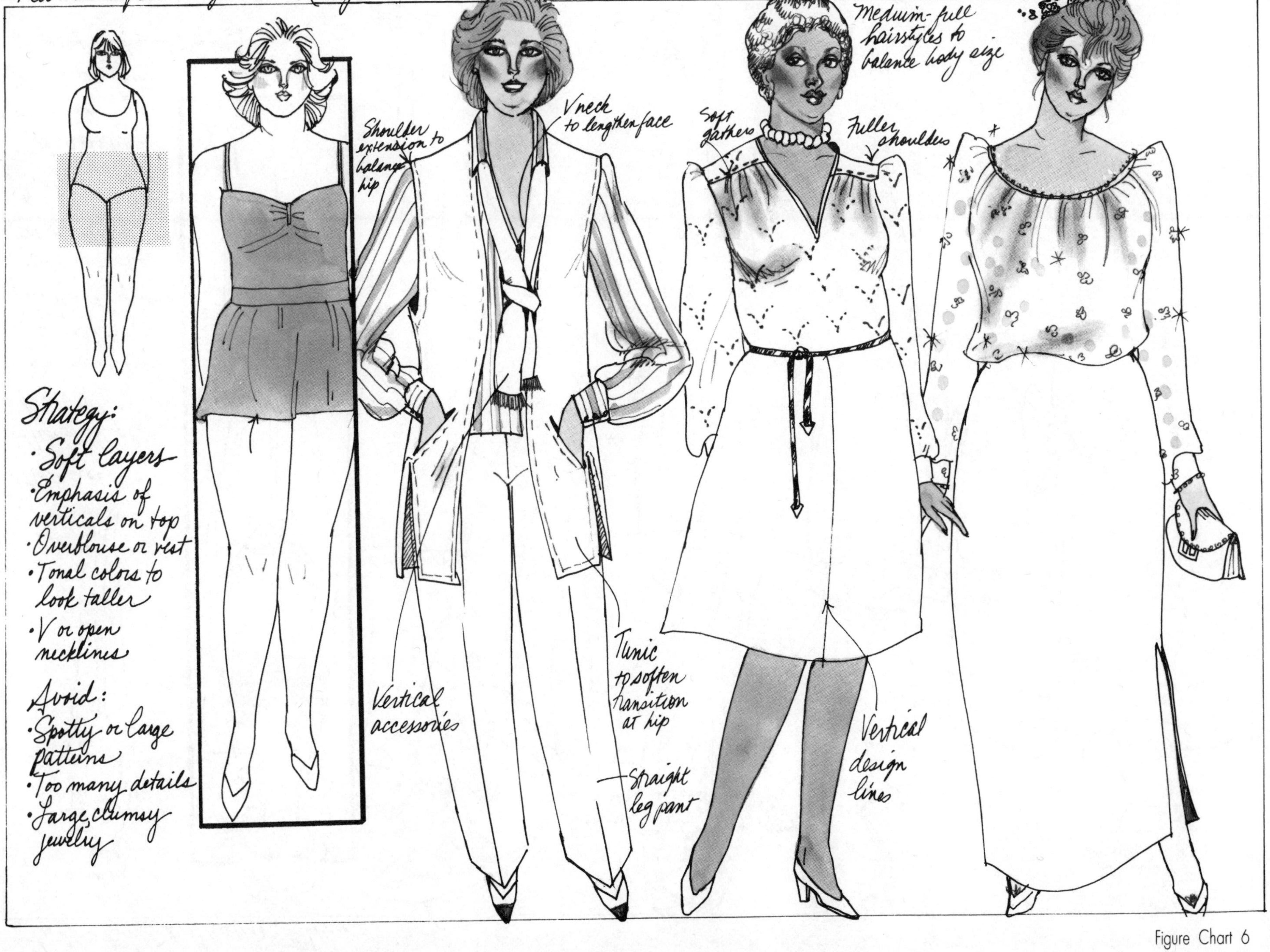
Shoulder extension to balance hip
V neck to lengthen face
Soft gathers
Fuller shoulders
Medium-full hairstyles to balance body size
Strategy:
· Soft layers
· Emphasis of verticals on top
· Overblouse or vest
· Tonal colors to look taller
· V or open necklines
Avoid:
· Spotty or large patterns
· Too many details
· Large, clumsy jewelry
Vertical accessories
Tunic to soften transition at hip
Straight leg pant
Vertical design lines

Figure Chart 6

Full-Busted Figure: Thin

Hip drape and detail

Hip detail

Simple top

Soft, fuller skirt

Semour neckline

No breast pocket

Hip details

Soft pleat pant

Strategy:
• Hip interest
• Hip belts to lengthen waist
• Soft gathers or fullness at hipline
• Low belts or hip design interest

Avoid:
• Full handras
• Smocks
• Very wide belts
• Brightly patterned tops

Figure Chart 7

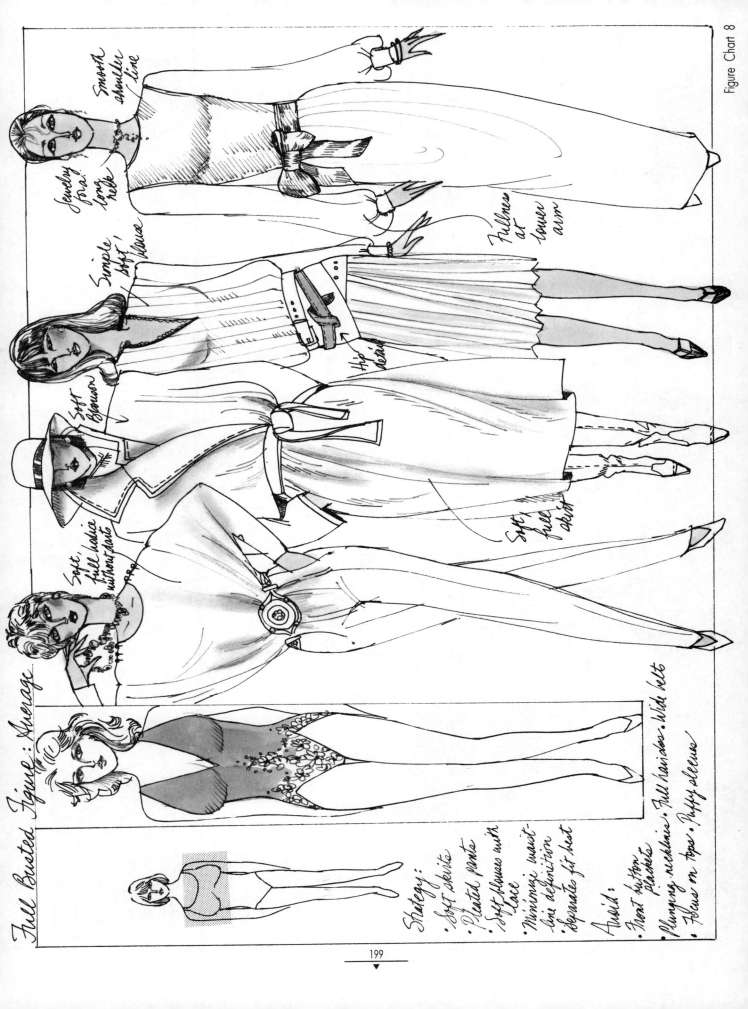

Full Busted Figure: Average

Smooth shoulder line

Sewing detail, long pull

Simple skirt, blouse

Fullness at lower arm

Soft blouson

Hip detail

Soft, full blouse without darts

Soft, full-line dress

Figure Chart 8

Strategy:
• Soft skirts
• Pleated pants
• Soft blouses with lace
• Minimize waist-line definition
• Separate fit best

Avoid:
• Front button placket
• Plunging necklines • Full hairdos • Wide belts
• Focus on tops • Puffy sleeves

199

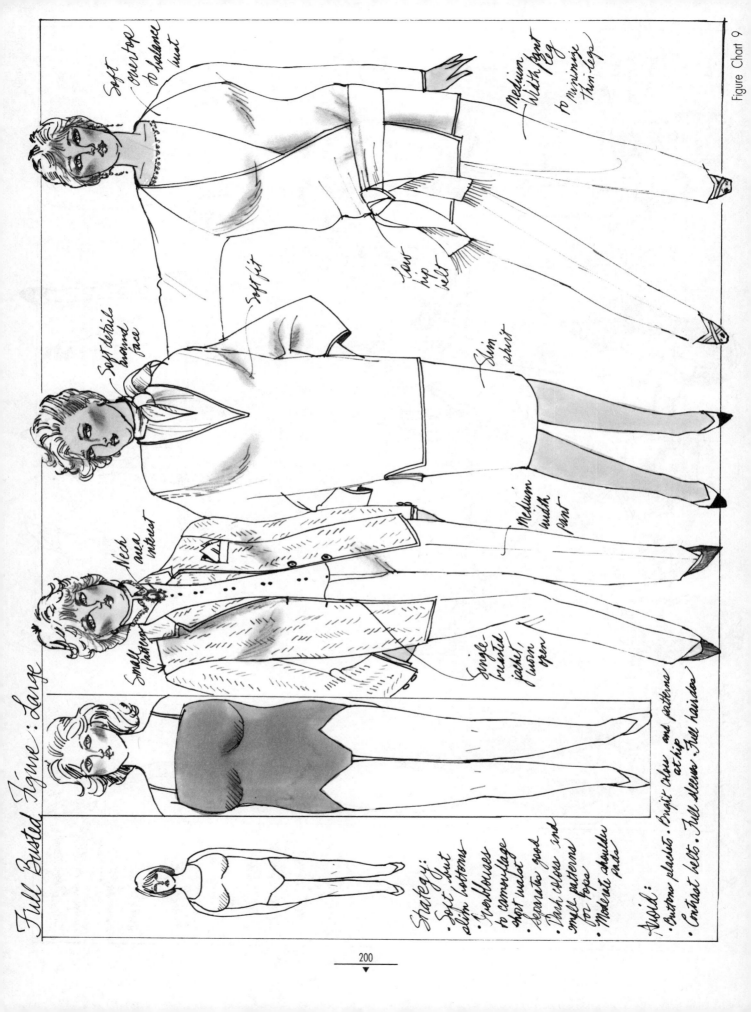

Full Busted Figure : Large

Soft overtop to balance bust

Soft detail around face

Neck area interest

Small pattern

Soft fit

Slim skirt

Medium width pant

Single-breasted jacket, worn open

Low hip belt

Medium width tight leg to minimize thin leg

Strategy:
· Soft shirt
· Slim bottoms
· Overblouses to camouflage short waist
· Seams to good
· Dark colour and small patterns to hide
· Moderate shoulder pads

Avoid:
· Buttons plackets · Bright colour and patterns at hip
· Contrast belts · Full sleeves · Full hairdos

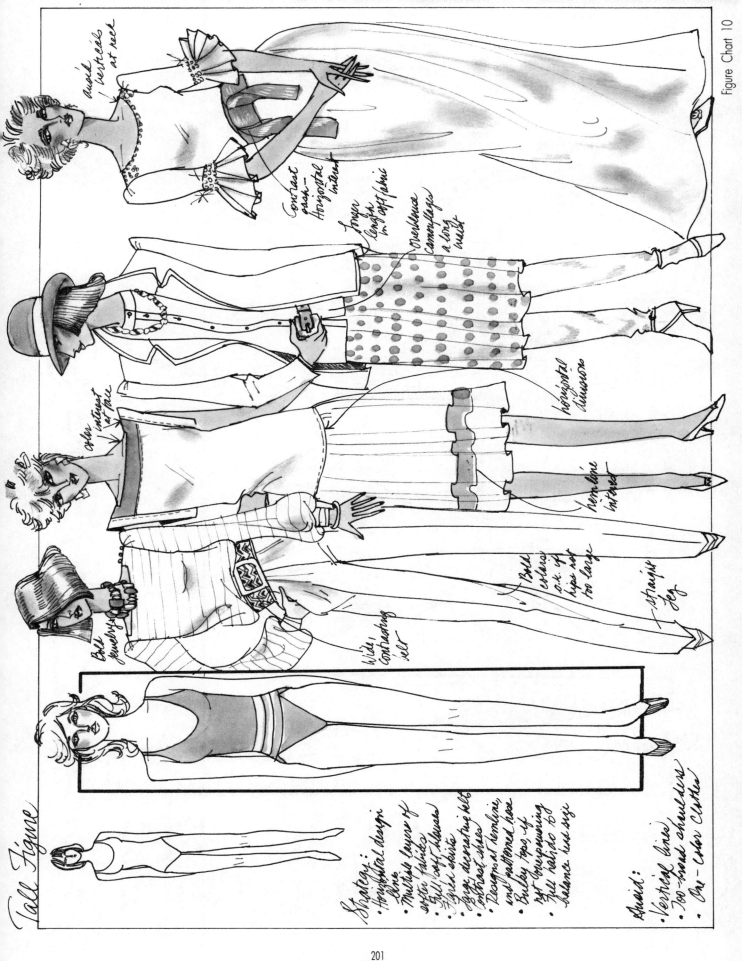

Tall Figure

Figure Chart 10

Strategy:
- Horizontal design line
- Multiple layers of softer fabric
- Full, soft blouses
- Broken lines
- Eye-arresting belts, contrast shoes
- Dropped hemline, unmatched hose
- Bulky tops if not overpowering
- Full skirts to balance hip size

Avoid:
- Vertical lines
- Too-small shoulders
- One-color clothes

Contrast pant - horizontal interest

Longer length in soft fabric

Overblouse camouflages a long waist

Color interest at face

Bold jewelry at face

Wide, contrasting belt

Bold colors o.k. if hips not too large

horizontal dimension

hemline interest

straight leg

avoid vertical interest at neck

Petite Figure

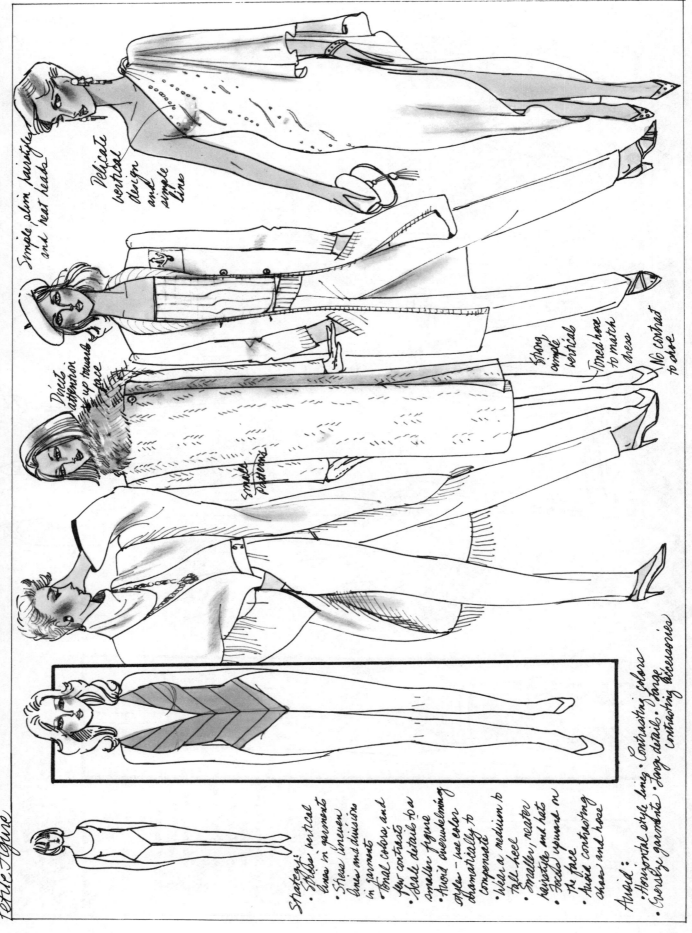

Delicate vertical design and simple line

Simple slim hairstyle and neat heels

Don't attention up towards face

Strong simple vertical

Toned hose to match dress

No contrast to shoe

Small Pattern

Strategy:
- Stress vertical lines in garment
- Stress uneven lines and divisions in garment
- Tonal colors and few contrasts
- Scale details to a smaller figure
- Avoid overwhelming styles - use color dramatically to compensate
- Wear a medium to tall heel
- Smaller, neater hairstyle and hat
- Focus upward in to the face
- Avoid contrasting shoes and hose

Avoid:
- Horizontal style lines • Contrasting colors
- Oversize garments • Long details • Large contrasting accessories

Long Waisted

Strategy:
- Narrow trim belts, worn at the top of the hips
- Hip interest
- Tone the waist with a tunic or skirt
- Emphasize verticals
- Use a belt and a draped blouse that folds over self.

Avoid:
- Snugly fitted bodies
- Wide waist bands
- Contrasting belts
- Fitted suits

Strategy:
- Wear large belts
- Tone the waist with a tunic
- Wear darker glow on top
- Emphasize horizontals
- Balance top with a dark color if torso is longer than legs

Avoid:
- Tops that are too short
- Insignificant waist detail—accent or loose it—do not be neutral

Loose dress in an overdress

Moderate width

Wide, Contrasting belts

Figure Chart 12

203
▼

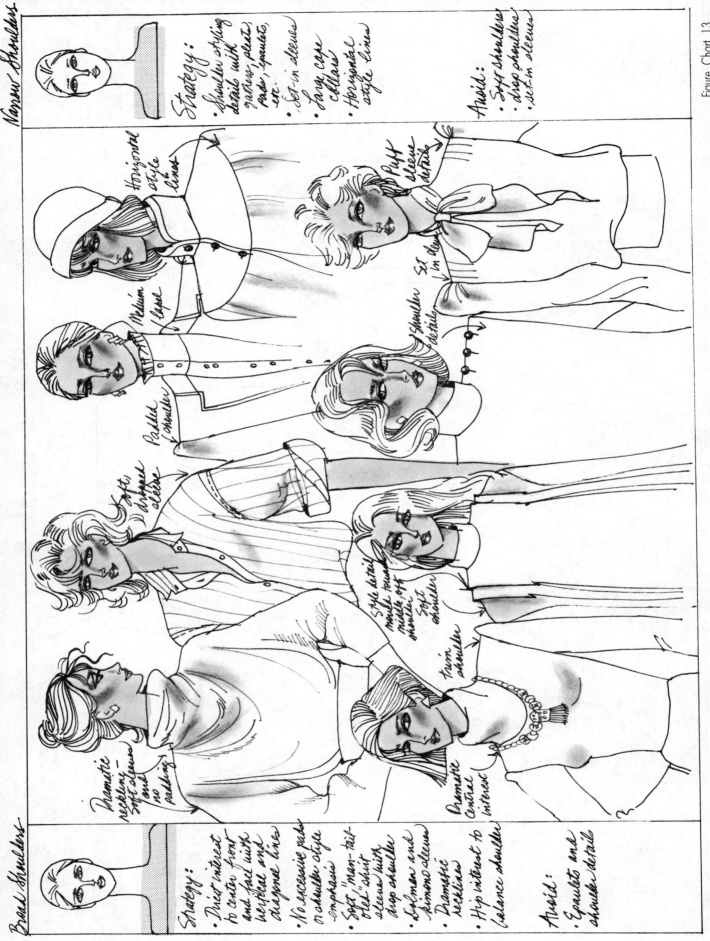

Figure Chart 13

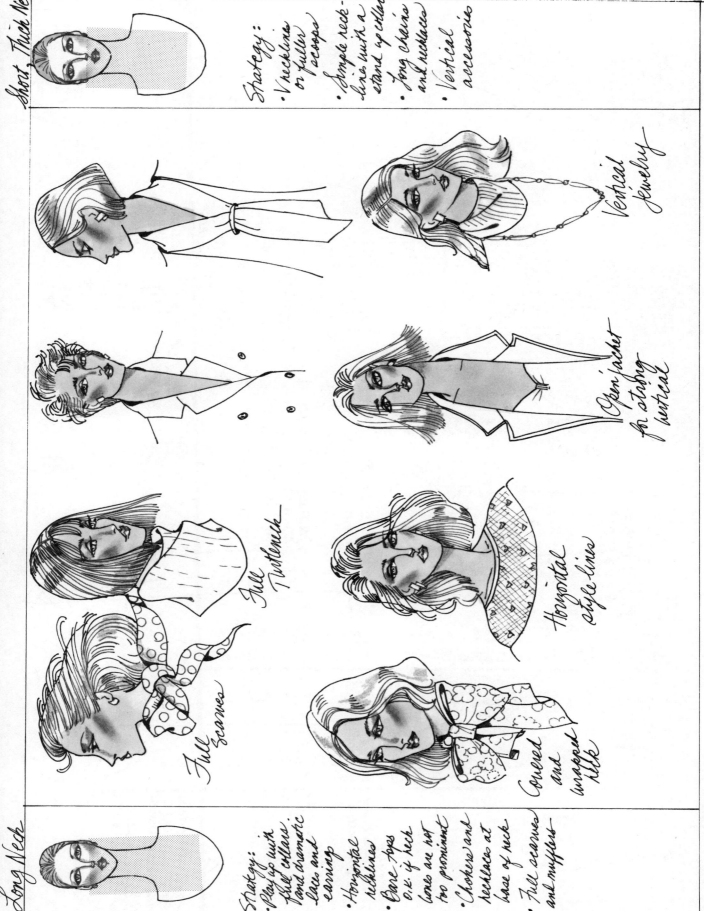

Pregnant Figure

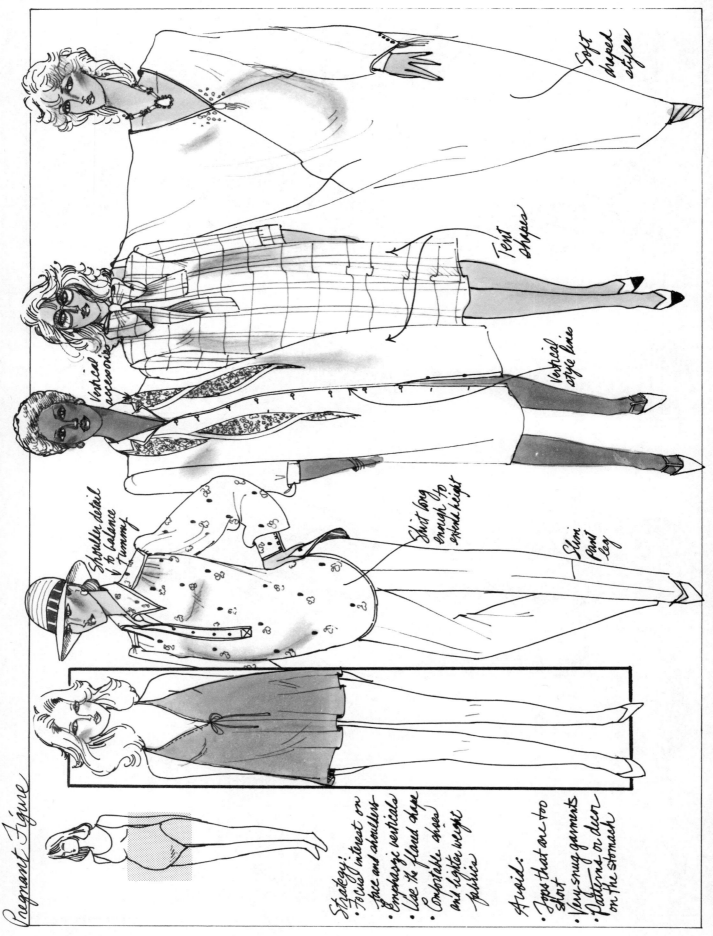

Soft draped styles

Tent shape

Vertical accessories

Vertical style line

Shoulder detail to balance Tummy

Shirt long enough to extend height

Slim Pant leg

Strategy:
• Focus interest on face and shoulders
• Emphasize verticals
• Use the flared shape
• Comfortable shoes and lighter weight fabrics

Avoid:
• Tops that are too short
• Very snug garments
• Patterns or color on the stomach

Attention: Every effort has been made to reproduce the colors on the facing page as accurately as possible. Due to the limitations of the four-color printing process, however, certain discrepancies are unavoidable. The color samples should therefore be used only as a guideline.